Spelling Workbook

Siegfried Engelmann

mheducation.com/prek-12

Copyright © 2021 McGraw-Hill Education

All rights reserved. No part of this publication may be reproduced or distributed in any form or by any means, or stored in a database or retrieval system, without the prior written consent of McGraw-Hill Education, including, but not limited to, network storage or transmission, or broadcast for distance learning.

Send all inquiries to:
McGraw-Hill Education
8787 Orion Place
Columbus, OH 43240

ISBN: 978-0-07-905384-8
MHID: 0-07-905384-X

Printed in the United States of America.

3 4 5 6 7 8 9 LMN 26 25 24 23 22

Name _____ **1**

A

Their report showed great imagination.

_____

B

1. acquire
2. deport
3. requirement   _____
4. eksport   _____
5. suported   _____
6. portable
7. imquire

C

In most words the morphograph **port** means "to carry." A port is a place where ships or airplanes pick up things and carry them away. If something is portable, it can be carried. A portable television is one that you can carry. The word **portable** is made of the morphographs **port** and **able**.

Port means "to carry." **Able** means "can be." So the word **portable** means "can be carried."

Things that are imported are carried into countries or places. The word **import** is made of the morphographs **im** and **port**.

Im means "in." **Port** means "to carry." So the word **import** means "to carry in."

In some words the meaning of **port** is more difficult to see. The word **important** comes from the word **import**. A long time ago the things imported into countries were very valuable. These things were called **important**, which means they were valuable. Later the word **important** came to mean "having great value."

Lesson 1   1

1. The morphograph **er,** which means "one who," is often added to the end of words. What word would mean **"one who carries things"**?

   _____

2. A foundation of a building is **under** the building. It **carries** the weight of the building. These morphographs mean "under": **sub, suc, sup, sur, sug, suf.** Which one goes with the morphograph **port** to tell what a foundation does for the rest of the building?

   _____

3. Goods **carried out of** a country are exported. What does the morphograph **ex** mean?

   _____

4. **Trans** means "across." What word means **"carry across land or water"**?

   _____

D Write the morphographs for each word.

1. _____ + _____ = portable
2. _____ + _____ + _____ + _____ = unreported
3. _____ + _____ = inquire
4. _____ + _____ = telegraph
5. _____ + _____ + _____ = photographic
6. _____ + _____ = acquire

END OF LESSON 1

Name _____

A
_____

B Write the morphographs for each word. If you are not sure of a spelling, use Word Parts.

1. _____ + _____ + _____ = photographer
2. _____ + _____ + _____ + _____ = misinformed
3. _____ + _____ + _____ = informal
4. _____ + _____ + _____ = performance
5. _____ + _____ = require
6. _____ + _____ + _____ = important

C The morphograph **port** means "to carry." Below are some words that use the morphograph **port**.

1. **export:** When goods are carried out of a country, those goods are exported.
2. **portable:** Something that can be carried is portable.
3. **transport:** When you transport something, you carry it across land, water, or air.
4. **support:** When you support something, you carry the weight or hold it up.
5. **important:** Something that is valuable is important.
6. **airport:** An airport is a place where things are carried in or out by aircraft.
7. **report:** When you report on something, you carry information back.

Lesson 2

Use the words with port to complete these sentences.

1. Maria said she wants to talk with you right away. She said it's very _____.

2. Japan does not import half as many things as it _____.

3. Kim wants to _____ the packages by train, but I think they would arrive sooner if they were shipped by air.

4. My television is too big to take with me wherever I go. I would rather have a _____ television.

5. The building is going to collapse unless we can _____ the first floor.

6. My flight leaves in an hour. Can you drive me to the _____?

7. He wrote a _____ on Spain that was very informative.

D

1. misspell
2. morphograph   _____
3. photograf   _____
4. telagraph   _____
5. misstaken
6. misjudged

E

1. t ____   4. l ____   7. p ____   10. o ____
2. e ____   5. u ____   8. a ____   11. b ____
3. n ____   6. i ____   9. d ____   12. e ____

END OF LESSON 2

Lesson 2

Name _____

A

_____

B

1. a _____
2. c _____
3. i _____
4. s _____
5. u _____
6. d _____
7. p _____
8. v _____
9. e _____
10. u _____
11. n _____
12. t _____

C

1. replace + ing = _____
2. replace + ment = _____
3. forgive + en = _____
4. like + ly = _____
5. use + age = _____
6. change + ing = _____
7. use + ful = _____
8. like + ness = _____
9. wide + est = _____
10. trace + ing = _____
11. bare + ly = _____
12. reuse + able = _____

Lesson 3

D

1. The first morphograph in the word **introduce** is either **in** or **intro**.
   Use Word Parts to find the correct morphograph. Then write the morphographs.

   _____ + _____ = introduce

2. The first morphograph in the word **across** is either **a** or **ac**. Use Word Parts.
   Then write the morphographs.

   _____ + _____ = across

3. The last morphograph in the word **action** is either **tion** or **ion**. Use Word Parts.
   Then write the morphographs.

   _____ + _____ = action

4. The first morphograph in the word **wonderful** is either **won** or **wonder**.
   Use Word Parts. Then write the morphographs.

   _____ + _____ = wonderful

E Three of these words are misspelled. Use Word Parts if you are not sure of the correct spellings. Write the misspelled words correctly on the lines.

1. formmal
2. telegraph   _____
3. reformed   _____
4. akquire   _____
5. transsport
6. greatly

END OF LESSON 3

Lesson 3

Name _____

A

1. _____
2. _____

B

1. hope + ing   = _____
2. hope + ful   = _____
3. late + ly   = _____
4. decide + ed = _____
5. expense + ive = _____
6. love + ly   = _____
7. mistake + en = _____
8. require + ment = _____
9. fine + al   = _____
10. fame + ous = _____

C

1. The second morphograph in the word **fortunate** is either **un** or **une.**
   Use Word Parts to find the correct morphograph. Then write the morphographs.

   _____ + _____ + _____ = fortunate

2. The second morphograph in the word **discontent** is either **con** or **co.** Use Word Parts.

   _____ + _____ + _____ = discontent

3. The last morphograph in the word **uncover** is either **er** or **cover.** Use Word Parts.

   _____ + _____ = uncover

4. The second morphograph in the word **television** is either **vise** or **vis.** Use Word Parts.

   _____ + _____ + _____ = television

D

snap   art   civil   trim

E

likely	morphograph	introduce	requirement
should	misspell	performance	usable
telegraph	acquire	transmit	support
forgiven	television	really	translate
useful	photographic	imagination	important
reported	formal	misinformed	hopelessly
	great	inquire	

Lesson 4

F The morphograph **graph** means "something in writing" or "something that is drawn." Below are some words that use the morphograph **graph**.

biography: **Bio** means "life." When you write a story about someone's life, you write a biography.

autobiography: **Auto** means "self." An autobiography is a biography you write about yourself.

morphograph: **Morpho** means "the form of something." So a morphograph is the written form of a word part.

autograph: Another word for your signature is your autograph.

graph: A graph is a drawing or a chart.

graphic: If something is graphic, it is like a graph. A drawing is a graphic. When you describe something in graphic detail, your description is as clear as a drawing.

Write the morphographs for each word.

1. _____ + _____ = graphic
2. _____ + _____ + _____ = biography
3. _____ + _____ = autograph
4. _____ + _____ + _____ + _____ = autobiography
5. What does the morphograph **auto** mean? _____

Write the correct words containing graph.

6. After she became rich and famous, she wrote her _____ .
7. I asked a film star to write her _____ inside my book.
8. Gil read a _____ about Winston Churchill.
9. They described the play in _____ detail.

Lesson 5 is a test lesson. There is no worksheet.

A

1. plan
2. rest
3. winter
4. big
5. step
6. port
7. brother
8. ship
9. earn

B

Use Word Parts to find the correct morphographs for each word. Write the morphographs below.

1. The last morphograph in the word **surprise** is either **ise** or **prise**.

   _____ + _____ = surprise

2. The last morphograph in the word **interest** is either **est** or **rest**.

   _____ + _____ = interest

C

In Lesson 4 you learned that the morphograph **graph** refers to something in writing or something that is drawn. Here are other words that contain **graph**.

graphite: Pencil lead is graphite.

telegraph: The morphograph **tele** means "distance." A telegraph sends messages over long distances.

photograph: The morphograph **photo** means "light." Photographs are pictures made with light.

geography: The morphograph **geo** means "earth." When you study geography, you study drawings or maps of Earth.

bibliography: The morphograph **biblio** means "book." A list of books used in writing an article is called a bibliography.

Write the morphographs for each word.

1. _____ + _____ + _____ = photography
2. _____ + _____ + _____ = geography
3. _____ + _____ = telegraph
4. _____ + _____ + _____ = bibliography

Lesson 6

Answer the items.

5. What does the morphograph **photo** mean? _____

6. What does the morphograph **tele** mean? _____

7. I am learning a lot about Earth's surface in my _____ class.

8. The word **photo** is a shorter word for _____.

9. The lead in my pencil is made of _____.

10. There is a long _____ at the end of the book.

D Add the morphographs together. Remember to use the final-e rule.

1. change + ing = _____
2. trade + s = _____
3. tele + scope = _____
4. con + fuse + ion = _____
5. value + able = _____
6. base + ment = _____

E Four of these words are misspelled. Use Word Parts if you are not sure of the correct spellings. Write the misspelled words correctly on the lines.

1. geographer
2. preformance
3. across
4. civelize
5. hopelesly
6. transmit
7. replacement
8. autograf

END OF LESSON 6

Lesson 6

7 Name _____

A

B

criticism   pleasure   notice   stranger   translation

C Add the morphographs together. Remember to use the doubling rule.

1. part + ing   = _____
2. pat + ing   = _____
3. bag + age   = _____
4. knot + s   = _____
5. form + al   = _____
6. mad + ness   = _____
7. pack + age   = _____
8. got + en   = _____

D

Last Saturday, my family went to see a new play. It was realy bad. A man interduced the play before it startted. He said we would have to use our imaginasions, but the play was hopeles.

All the actors gave terrible preformances. Nobody understood the story. I wish we had stayed home and watched teluvision.

E Use Word Parts to find the correct morphographs for each word. Write the morphographs below.

1. The first morpograph in the word **pleasure** is either **please** or **plea**.

   _____ + _____ = pleasure

2. The second morphograph in the word **transmission** is either **miss** or **mis**.

   _____ + _____ + _____ = transmission

3. The first morphograph in the word **dispel** is either **dis** or **di**.

   _____ + _____ = dispel

F Add the morphographs together. Remember to use the final-e rule.

1. pulse + ate = _____

2. in + quire + ing = _____

3. white + est = _____

4. base + ic = _____

5. ex + press + ive = _____

6. athlete + ic = _____

7. value + less = _____

8. store + age = _____

END OF LESSON 7

Lesson 7   13

8

Name _____

A
_____

_____

B

partial   athletically   deduction   excessively   critically

C Add the morphographs together. Remember to use the doubling rule.

1. sad + ness = _____
2. wash + er = _____
3. spot + ed = _____
4. magic + al = _____
5. hat + s = _____
6. critic + ism = _____
7. trip + ed = _____
8. civil + ize = _____

D

The origin of a word is the place the word originally came from. The word **tea** originally came from China, which is where people first got tea leaves. The Chinese word for tea is **te**. When English people took over the word, they changed the word to **tea**. Many English words have foreign origins, like the word **tea**. But very few words come from Chinese.

Most English words follow the same pattern of origin. These words were first in Greek. Then they went to Latin. Then they went to French. And finally, they became part of English. Greek is the language spoken in Greece and is over three thousand years old. Latin is the language that people used to speak in Italy. French is the language that people speak in France.

The Greeks were very smart. They made up many words and ideas. The people in Italy admired the Greeks and copied what they did. Italian people often copied Greek words. They changed the words a little bit, but the Latin words were clearly copies of the Greek words.

When people from Italy moved into France, they took the Latin language with them. The French people changed the Latin words and changed the spelling.

When these words come into English, they are Greek words that have been changed somewhat when they went into Latin and changed again when they went into French. Sometimes their spelling and pronunciation change again as the word becomes an English word.

Answer the items.

1. Where was Latin spoken? _____
2. Where is French spoken? _____
3. Is Latin still spoken today? _____
4. What is the origin of a word? _____
5. Where does the word **tea** come from? _____
6. From whom did the Italians copy words? _____

Lesson 8

E A student wrote this letter. The letter contains nine misspelled words. Write each of those words correctly. If you're not sure of a word, look it up in Word Parts.

Dear Grandmother,

    Last Friday was the last day of shcool, so our famly will be comming to visit you soon. On Friday, we had a spelling contest in our class, and my best freind won! I did okay at first, but the spelings got too hard, and I made a misstake trying to spell ATHLETIC, so I was out of the contest. Connie did'nt mispell a single word, including the last one, which was DINOSAUR, so she won a realy nice dictionary.

    See you next week!

Love,

Bernice

END OF LESSON 8

Name _____

A
_____

B

1. _____   4. _____
2. _____   5. _____
3. _____   6. _____

C

admirable   medicine   physicist   amusement   photography

D Write the morphographs for each word. Figure out any morphographs you don't know. Use Word Parts.

1. fort + _____ + _____ = fortunate
2. in + _____ + _____ = inversion
3. _____ + _____ + ion = television
4. per + _____ + _____ = perceptive
5. _____ + _____ + ly = critically

Lesson 9   17

E Four of these words are misspelled. Use Word Parts to find the correct spellings. Write the misspelled words correctly.

1. finaly
2. unbreakable
3. partial   _____
4. preformance   _____
5. intermission   _____
6. atheletically   _____
7. excessively
8. deduction
9. supervizion

F Add the morphographs together. Remember to use the doubling rule.

1. sit + ing   = _____
2. wonder + ful   = _____
3. real + ize   = _____
4. snap + ed   = _____
5. star + less   = _____
6. swim + er   = _____
7. hot + est   = _____
8. poison + ous   = _____

G People who lived in Italy used to speak Latin. Those people were called Romans. The Romans used the Roman alphabet to spell Latin words. The 26-letter English alphabet comes from the Roman alphabet. The Roman alphabet comes from the 24-letter Greek alphabet.

So a lot of the letters in our alphabet came first from Greek, then from Latin, and finally into English.

Some letters of the alphabet have an interesting history. The word **alphabet** is made up of the first two letters of the Greek alphabet. These letters are **alpha** (A, α) and **beta** (B, β). You can hear them in the word **alphabet.**

A letter that has an interesting history is **c.** The Greeks did not have a letter **c.** Neither did the Romans. The Romans had a letter for the **g** sound that looked like this: G, g. They changed it to look like this for the **k** sound: C, c.

The letter **c** makes two sounds in English—the sound like an **s** (as in **cell**) and the sound like **k** (as in **cup**). Since English already has a symbol for the **k** sound (k) and a symbol for the **s** sound (s), we really don't need the symbol **c.** But this symbol is very important to our spelling. Here is why: Some morphographs are pronounced in different ways when they are combined with other morphographs. However, the morphographs are always spelled the same way. The letter **c** can stand for the **s** sound or the **k** sound. So we can spell words like **medic** and **medicine** with the same spelling. If we didn't have the letter **c,** we would have to spell the words this way: **medik, medisine.**

So this is how we got our ABCs. Our **A** and **B** came from Greek, and our **C** came from the Romans.

Below are the letters from the Greek alphabet. After each number write the English letter.

Here's a hint: **Lambda** is **l,** and **Mu** is **m.**

    Λ, λ (lambda)   =   l

    M, μ (mu)   =   m

You can figure out the letters by looking at them.

1. **O, o** (omicron) = _____

2. **T, τ** (tau) = _____

3. **B, β** (beta) = _____

4. **E, ε** (epsilon) = _____

5. **A, α** (alpha) = _____

Answer the items.

6. From what words did the word **alphabet** come? _____

7. Did the letter **c** come from Greek or Latin? _____

8. What sound does the **c** in **physic** make when you add **ist**? _____

9. What sound does the **c** in **physic** make when you add **al**? _____

10. What sound does the first **c** in **criticize** make? _____

11. What sound does the second **c** in **criticize** make? _____

12. What are the morphographs in **criticize**? _____

Lesson 10 is a test lesson. There is no worksheet.

Name _____ **11**

A

1. _____
2. _____

B

revision   thorough   through   embarrassed   infection

C Make 9 real words from the morphographs in the box.

| ly | er | sore | strange | est | ness | sad |

1. _____   6. _____
2. _____   7. _____
3. _____   8. _____
4. _____   9. _____
5. _____

D Circle all the words that end in a consonant and the letter **y**.

1. study   5. enjoy   9. they
2. play   6. spray   10. pity
3. toy   7. cry   11. relay
4. marry   8. happy   12. nasty

Lesson 11   **21**

E Write the correct spelling for each word in the word column.
Then write **O**, **A**, or **B** after each number in the rule column:

Write **O** if the word is spelled by just putting the morphographs together.
Write **A** if the final-**e** rule explains why the spelling is changed.
Write **B** if the doubling rule explains why the spelling is changed.

	rule		word
1.	_____	ship + ing =	_____
2.	_____	race + ing =	_____
3.	_____	hope + less =	_____
4.	_____	hope + ful =	_____
5.	_____	star + less =	_____
6.	_____	run + er =	_____
7.	_____	re + fine + ing =	_____
8.	_____	verse + ion =	_____

F Write the morphographs for each word. Figure out any morphographs you don't know. Use Word Parts.

1. im + _____ + _____ = impartial
2. _____ + _____ = failure
3. _____ + _____ + ledge = acknowledge
4. _____ + _____ = justice

END OF LESSON 11

Name

A

1. play + ful = _____
2. pity + ful = _____
3. try + ed = _____
4. try + ing = _____
5. toy + s = _____
6. study + ing = _____
7. vary + ed = _____
8. glory + ous = _____
9. heavy + est = _____
10. joy + ous = _____

B

1. _____
2. _____
3. _____
4. _____
5. _____
6. _____
7. _____
8. _____
9. _____
10. _____
11. _____
12. _____
13. _____
14. _____
15. _____

C Add the morphographs together. Remember to use your spelling rules.
The morphograph u is a vowel letter.

1. fat + y = _____
2. blame + less = _____
3. in + cure + able = _____
4. ease + y = _____
5. mis + take + en = _____
6. run + y = _____
7. hope + ful = _____
8. im + prove + ed = _____
9. store + age = _____
10. shine + y = _____

D Make 9 real words from the morphographs in the box.

| ing | bag | store | age | ed | lack | pack |

1. _____   6. _____
2. _____   7. _____
3. _____   8. _____
4. _____   9. _____
5. _____

E Write the correct spelling for each word in the word column.
Then write **O**, **A**, or **B** after each number in the rule column:

Write **O** if the word is spelled by just putting the morphographs together.
Write **A** if the final-**e** rule explains why the spelling is changed.
Write **B** if the doubling rule explains why the spelling is changed.

	rule		word
1.	_____	care + less =	_____
2.	_____	fate + al =	_____
3.	_____	plan + ing =	_____
4.	_____	move + ment =	_____
5.	_____	slam + ed =	_____
6.	_____	judge + ing =	_____
7.	_____	shop + er =	_____
8.	_____	mad + ness =	_____

END OF LESSON 12

Name _____

A

B

1. stay + ing = _____
2. hurry + ing = _____
3. fancy + est = _____
4. worry + ed = _____
5. enjoy + ment = _____
6. beauty + ful = _____
7. cry + ing = _____
8. say + ing = _____

C A student wrote this report. The report contains seven misspelled words. Write each of those words correctly.

    Many experts agree that spelling is an important skill for students to have. If a student mispells words in a written report, peopel reading the report tend to judge that the report is poor, even if the content of the report is excellent and is presented well. Sum geografy teachers have been known to fail students for poor spelling. Many teachers do not fail students but reqire correct spelling on all reportes.

_____
_____
_____
_____
_____
_____
_____

26 Lesson 13

D We use paragraphs to show when writing goes from one topic to another. People didn't always use paragraphs, however. The Greeks who wrote over two thousand years ago completely covered the page with writing. There were no spaces between the lines, no commas, and no periods. When they switched topics, they wouldn't indent and start a new paragraph. They made a small mark next to that line. They called this mark a **paragraph.**

The word **paragraph** is made up of two morphographs — **para** and **graph. Para** means "next to." **Graph** means "something written."

Today we usually indent the first line of a new topic instead of writing a little mark beside it. But sometimes we show a new paragraph by skipping a line so that extra space is created between topics. The word **paragraph** is still with us to refer to a change in topic.

1. Name three ways the early Greek writing was different from ours. _____

2. What does the morphograph **para** mean? _____

3. What does the morphograph **graph** mean? _____

4. How did Greek writers show a change of topic? _____

5. How do we show a change of topic today? _____

E **Write the morphographs for each word. Figure out any morphographs you don't know. Use Word Parts.**

1. _____ + _____ + ual + _____ = unusually
2. _____ + _____ + ed = diseased
3. manu + _____ + _____ = manufacture
4. _____ + _____ + ion = admission

Lesson 13   **27**

F Write the correct spelling for each word in the word column.
Then write O, A, or B after each number in the rule column:

Write **O** if the word is spelled by just putting the morphographs together.
Write **A** if the final-**e** rule explains why the spelling is changed.
Write **B** if the doubling rule explains why the spelling is changed.

	rule		word
1.	_____	friend + ly =	_____
2.	_____	please + ure =	_____
3.	_____	step + ed =	_____
4.	_____	ap + pear + ance =	_____
5.	_____	fort + une + ate =	_____
6.	_____	skin + y =	_____

END OF LESSON 13

Name

A

B

visitor   television   devise   bury   deny

C

1. _____   4. _____
2. _____   5. _____
3. _____

D

Make 7 real words from the morphographs in the box.

| mis | en | hap | take | s |

1. _____   5. _____
2. _____   6. _____
3. _____   7. _____
4. _____

E The morphograph **vise** usually means "to see." Below are some words that use the morphograph **vise**.

visit: When you go to see friends or relatives, you visit them.

supervisor: Someone who is responsible for watching over the work of others is a supervisor.

visible: A visible thing is something you can see.

advise: When you help people solve a problem, you advise them. You help them see the problem more clearly.

television: **Tele** means "distance." A television permits us to see pictures sent over long distances.

revise: When you revise something you have written, you change it to make it better by seeing it again.

Write the morphographs for each word.

1. _____ + _____ = vision
2. _____ + _____ + _____ = advised
3. _____ + _____ = devise
4. _____ + _____ = televise
5. _____ + it + _____ = visitor
6. _____ + _____ + _____ = revision

Answer these items.

7. Something that is not visible is **invisible**. What does the morphograph **in** mean in this word? _____

8. A visitor is one who visits you. A supervisor is one who supervises you. What does the morphograph **or** mean? _____

Write the correct words containing vise.

9. Mrs. McAllister is working on the second _____ of the cookbook she is writing.

10. Freddy needs new contact lenses because his _____ is poor.

11. Marsha _____ me to begin my book report right away.

12. I wonder if any network is going to _____ the world soccer championships.

F **Add the morphographs together. Remember to use your spelling rules.**

1. play + ful = _____
2. sturdy + est = _____
3. marry + ed = _____
4. deny + al = _____
5. copy + ed = _____
6. hap + y + ness = _____
7. carry + age = _____
8. bury + ed = _____
9. dry + ing = _____
10. try + al = _____

Lesson 15 is a test lesson. There is no worksheet.

16   Name _____

A

B   Three of these words are misspelled. Use Word Parts to find the correct spellings. Write the misspelled words correctly.

1. embarassed
2. paragraph
3. revision
4. easiest
5. burial
6. thorough
7. visitor
8. appeer
9. critisize

C   Write the morphographs for each word. Figure out any morphographs you don't know. Use Word Parts.

1. _____ + _____ + ary = imaginary
2. _____ + _____ + _____ + _____ = informative
3. _____ + _____ + ant = unpleasant
4. _____ + _____ = paragraph

D

Add the morphographs together. Remember to use your spelling rules. The morphograph y is a vowel letter.

1. noise + y + er = _____
2. com + mit + ment = _____
3. hap + en = _____
4. busy + ness = _____
5. en + joy + ed = _____
6. per + hap + s = _____
7. use + ual = _____
8. in + vise + ible = _____
9. strange + ly = _____
10. o + mit = _____
11. hap + y + ly = _____
12. super + vise + ion = _____

E

Write the word for each meaning clue.

> visible   advise   supervisor

1. someone who is responsible for watching over the work of others _____
2. can be seen _____
3. to help someone solve a problem _____

END OF LESSON 16

17 Name _____

A

1. _____
2. _____

B Make 12 real words from the morphographs in the box.
The letter x acts like two consonant letters.

| y | sun | wax | luck | wit | er | hap | est |

1. _____   7. _____
2. _____   8. _____
3. _____   9. _____
4. _____   10. _____
5. _____   11. _____
6. _____   12. _____

C

Some morphographs have more than one meaning. The morphograph **sent** has three different meanings.

One meaning of **sent** is "to send in the past": We sent the package yesterday. We will send another one tomorrow.

Another meaning of **sent** is "to feel." The word **consent** has this meaning. When you **consent** to something, you feel that it is all right to do. The words re**sent**, dis**sent**, and **sent**imental also have the meaning "to feel."

Another meaning of **sent** is "to exist." The morphograph **ab** means "away." When you are absent, you are not here. You exist away from here. The opposite of **absent** is **present.** **Pre** means "in front of." When you are present, you are in front of us.

34 Lesson 17

Match the correct meaning of <u>sent</u> for each underlined word.

> feeling   exist   send in the past

1. I <u>resent</u> her coming here.   _____
2. Acme Company <u>sent</u> us the bill last week.   _____
3. Susie was <u>present</u> at the meeting.   _____
4. He is very <u>sentimental</u> about his past.   _____
5. My mother never <u>consents</u> to letting me stay out late.   _____
6. Yesterday no one was <u>absent</u> from class.   _____

D Write the correct spelling for each word in the <u>word</u> column. Then write <u>O</u>, <u>A</u>, <u>B</u>, or <u>C</u> after each number in the <u>rule</u> column:

Write **O** if the word is spelled by just putting the morphographs together.
Write **A** if the final-**e** rule explains why the spelling is changed.
Write **B** if the doubling rule explains why the spelling is changed.
Write **C** if the **y**-to-**i** rule explains why the spelling is changed.

rule   **word**

1. _____ hazard + ous = _____
2. _____ hap + en = _____
3. _____ athlete + ic + s = _____
4. _____ bury + al = _____
5. _____ re + place + ment = _____
6. _____ hurry + ing = _____
7. _____ swim + er = _____
8. _____ in + quire + ed = _____

END OF LESSON 17

18 Name _____

A

1. _____
2. _____
   _____
3. _____
   _____
4. _____
   _____

B
Write the correct word for each sentence. If you are not sure of a word, look it up in the list of homonyms in the back of your workbook.

1. They made a **right/write** turn. _____
2. Look over **their/there**. _____
3. I can't **hear/here** you. _____
4. I have a **hole/whole** in my stocking. _____

C
Make 12 real words from the morphographs in the box.

| bake | shop | s | swim | er | wrap | ing |

1. _____   7. _____
2. _____   8. _____
3. _____   9. _____
4. _____   10. _____
5. _____   11. _____
6. _____   12. _____

36 Lesson 18

D Add the morphographs together. Remember to use your spelling rules.

1. cry + ing = _____
2. un + fix + ed = _____
3. hap + y = _____
4. embarrass + ment = _____
5. friend + ly + est = _____
6. per + mit = _____
7. copy + ing = _____
8. ac + know + ledge = _____
9. box + er = _____
10. manu + fact + ure + er = _____

E Write the correct spelling for each word in the word column. Then write **O**, **A**, **B**, or **C** after each number in the rule column:

Write **O** if the word is spelled by just putting the morphographs together.
Write **A** if the final-**e** rule explains why the spelling is changed.
Write **B** if the doubling rule explains why the spelling is changed.
Write **C** if the **y**-to-**i** rule explains why the spelling is changed.

rule   word

1. _____ stop + ing = _____
2. _____ deny + ing = _____
3. _____ please + ant = _____
4. _____ im + prove + ment = _____
5. _____ hid + en = _____
6. _____ worry + some = _____

END OF LESSON 18

19   Name _____

A

1. _____   6. _____
2. _____   7. _____
3. _____   8. _____
4. _____   9. _____
5. _____   10. _____

B   Write the correct word for each sentence. If you are not sure of a word, look it up in the list of homonyms in the back of your workbook.

1. Shawn can sing the **hole/whole** song.   _____

2. We walked **threw/through** the building.   _____

3. Bill told a very imaginative **tail/tale**.   _____

4. We know how to **sail/sale** a boat.   _____

5. Murry is asking the bank for a **loan/lone**.   _____

6. There is only one **peace/piece** of pie left.   _____

C A student wrote this report. The report contains eleven misspelled words. Write each of those words correctly. If you're not sure of a contraction, look it up in the list of contractions in the back of your workbook.

If you want to be an athlete, you have to work out every day. Swimming and runing are good exercises four improoving you're body. Atheletic activities dont' always reqwire grate phisical strength, but they do reqwire a lot of training.

_____

_____

_____

_____

_____

_____

_____

_____

_____

_____

_____

D Write the morphographs for each word. Figure out any morphographs you don't know. Use Word Parts.

1. _____ + com + _____ + _____ = accommodate

2. _____ + _____ = dispel

3. _____ + ual = casual

4. _____ + _____ = receive

Lesson 19

E The Greeks were superstitious. They believed that events could be predicted by studying the stars. Their morphographs for **star** are **aster** and **astro.**

The Greek word **astrology** means "the study of stars for predicting future events." An **astrologer** is not a scientist, but someone who tells future events by studying stars.

The scientific study of stars and planets is called **astronomy.** The morphograph **nome** means "to name." An **astronomer** is a scientist who identifies stars and other heavenly bodies. An astronomer can name the stars.

The Greeks thought that a disaster was caused by bad stars. Today we use the word **disaster** to mean "a terrible event."

The word **astronomical** means "extremely large" or "great, like the universe."

Answer the questions. You may use Word Parts.

1. Why do you think this punctuation mark * is called an asterisk? Write the morphographs for **asterisk** with plus signs.

   _____

2. Write the morphographs for **astronomy, astronomical**, and **astronomer.**

   _____

3. Is an **astrologer** a scientist? Is an **astronomer** a scientist?

   _____

4. The morphograph **naut** means "sailor." The morphograph **cosmo** means "world." Russian space travelers are called **cosmonauts.** The name for space travelers from the United States contains the Greek morphograph for **star.** What's the name?

   _____

5. If something is given the wrong name, it is called a **misnomer.** Write the morphographs for **misnomer.**

   _____

Lesson 20 is a test lesson. There is no worksheet.

Name _____

21

A

1. _____
2. _____
3. _____
4. _____

B Do not use Word Parts for Part B.

In 1613, a Dutch trading ship that was anchored near Manhattan Island caught fire. Attempts to save the ship failed, and the crew had to go ashore. Onshore, friendly Native Americans offered survivors food and shelter. Encouraged by the warm welcome, the Dutch decided to build their first colony on that site, which later became New York City.

Who were the first European settlers of New York City?

Some Duch traders had to abandon there burning ship, which was ankered near Manhattan Iland. Some freindly Native Americans gave food and shelter to the traders. The traders found the wellcome so encuraging that they desided to bild a collony, which became New York City.

_____
_____
_____
_____
_____
_____
_____
_____
_____

Lesson 21

C

**Write the correct spelling for each word in the word column.
Then write O, A, B or C after each number in the rule column:**

Write **O** if the word is spelled by just putting the morphographs together.
Write **A** if the final-**e** rule explains why the spelling is changed.
Write **B** if the doubling rule explains why the spelling is changed.
Write **C** if the **y**-to-**i** rule explains why the spelling is changed.

	rule		word
1.	_____	oc + case + ion =	_____
2.	_____	cur + ent =	_____
3.	_____	fant + as + y =	_____
4.	_____	ad + vise + ed =	_____
5.	_____	oc + cur =	_____
6.	_____	deny + ing =	_____
7.	_____	plan + ed =	_____
8.	_____	vary + ous =	_____

D

Some words that contain an **f** sound in our language are spelled with the letters **ph**. These words come from Greek words, not from Latin words or French words. The words gra**ph**, **ph**oto, and s**ph**ere are words that come from Greek.

The reason these words are spelled with **ph** rather than **f** has to do with letters in the Greek alphabet. The symbol used for the **f** sound in the Greek Alphabet is Φ. The name of this symbol is **phi**.

When the Romans translated Greek symbols, they used the letters **ph** to stand for Φ. So words that have **ph** for the **f** sound come from Greek.

1. For each of the words below, write the morphographs that come from Greek. For example, the morphographs in **philosophy** that come from Greek are **philo** and **soph.**

   soph + ist + ic + ate + ed = sophisticated _____

   re + phrase = rephrase _____

   morpho + graph = morphograph _____

   physic + al = physical _____

2. The word **uphill** does not come from Greek. How do you know it's not Greek even though it has **ph?**

   _____

3. Sometimes the Romans would change the Greek **ph** spelling to **f.** The Greek morphograph **phant** means "something seen." The word **phantom** has the morphograph **phant.** Two of our English words used to be spelled **phantasy** and **phantastic.** Write the correct modern spelling of these two words that originally came from Greek.

   _____

4. The morphograph **phet** means "to speak" in the word **prophet.** The morphograph **fess** means "to speak" in the word **confess.** Which morphograph shows Latin spelling, **phet** or **fess?** Which morphograph shows Greek spelling?

   _____

5. Writing and drawing on walls has been going on for hundreds of years. The Romans called it **graffito.** The plural word for **graffito** is **graffiti.** What Greek morphograph means the same as Roman **graf?**

   _____

END OF LESSON 21

22

A

1. _____
2. _____
3. _____
   _____
4. _____

B Do not use Word Parts for Part B.

Wool was very important to the economy in England four hundred years ago. The king passed a law requiring everyone over the age of seven to wear a wool cap. This law was designed to sell more wool. Anyone who did not comply with the law was fined. Wool was so important to England that anyone selling sheep outside the country was punished by death.

Why were wool caps a common sight in England 400 years ago?

    Because of the econnomic importence of wool in England, the king past a law which recuired everyone to where a wool cap. This happened for hundred years ago. Being seen without one resulted in being find, so nearly everyone complyed with the law.

C Write the morphographs for each word. Figure out any morphographs you don't know. Use Word Parts.

1. mode + _____ + _____ = modernize
2. _____ + _____ = another
3. _____ + _____ + _____ = misfortune
4. _____ + _____ + _____ = philosopher
5. _____ + _____ + _____ = consistent
6. _____ + _____ + _____ + ate + _____ = accomodation
7. _____ + _____ = imagine
8. _____ + _____ = poisonous

D Write the correct word or words for each sentence. If you're not sure of a word, look it up in the list of homonyms in the back of your workbook.

1. A little **peace/piece** and quiet will do her good. _____
2. Cynthia bought some **plain/plane** white paper. _____
3. I wish she **wood/would right/write** to me. _____
4. **Meat/Meet** is **vary/very** expensive these days. _____

END OF LESSON 22

23   Name _____

A

By eating pears, he lost weight around his waist.

B Add the morphographs together. Remember to use your spelling rules.

1. cur + ent = _____
2. oc + case + ion + al + ly = _____
3. astro + nome + er = _____
4. com + mode + ity = _____
5. fant + as + y + es = _____
6. dure + ing = _____
7. re + phrase + ed = _____
8. ap + ply + ed = _____
9. hemi + sphere = _____
10. case + ual + ty = _____

C Write the correct word for each sentence. If you're not sure of a word, look it up in the list of homonyms in the back of your workbook.

1. Sally is learning how to fly a **plain/plane**. _____
2. **Where/Wear** are you going? _____
3. The dog chased its **tail/tale**. _____
4. The deer fled **threw/through** the forest. _____

46   Lesson 23

D **A student wrote this report. Seven words are misspelled. Write each of those words correctly.**

We viseted a great, beautyful hotel last summer. This hotel was a fashionable resort for people who like to go swimming and play tennis. The hotel was origenally built in 1890, but the acomodations were comfortable and moderne. We were required to wear formel clothes for the evening meal, but we didn't mind. It was fun. Unfortunatly, we made reservations for only two nights. I wish we could have stayed longer.

_____

_____

_____

_____

_____

_____

_____

END OF LESSON 23

24 Name

A

1. _____
2. _____
3. _____
4. _____
5. _____
6. _____
7. _____
8. _____
9. _____
10. _____
11. _____
12. _____
13. _____
14. _____
15. _____
16. _____
17. _____
18. _____
19. _____
20. _____

B Write the correct spelling for each word in the word column.
Then write O, A, B or C after each number in the rule column:

Write **O** if the word is spelled by just putting the morphographs together.
Write **A** if the final-**e** rule explains why the spelling is changed.
Write **B** if the doubling rule explains why the spelling is changed.
Write **C** if the **y**-to-**i** rule explains why the spelling is changed.

#	rule		word
1.	_____	act + ual + ly =	_____
2.	_____	knot + ed =	_____
3.	_____	like + ly + hood =	_____
4.	_____	verse + ion =	_____
5.	_____	in + con + sist + ent =	_____
6.	_____	en + dure + ance =	_____
7.	_____	com + ply + ing =	_____
8.	_____	step + ing =	_____
9.	_____	mode + er + ate =	_____
10.	_____	fun + y =	_____

C Write the correct word for each sentence. If you're not sure of a word, look it up in the list of homonyms in the back of your workbook.

1. I'm hoping that the **weather/whether** will change.   _____
2. He performed a daring **feat/feet**.   _____
3. We will **meat/meet** in another room.   _____
4. Where **wood/would** you like to sit?   _____

Lesson 24

D **Find the misspelled words in the student's answer. Then write them correctly. Do not use Word Parts.**

For years, industry emptied chemical waste of all types into the Cuyahoga River, which winds through Cleveland, Ohio, in the United States. Cleveland's residents occasionally complained about the river's vile condition, but nothing was done about it until 1969. In that year, the thick, oily surface of the river, littered with trash and rubble, caught fire, and the fire would not go out. The poisonous waterway blazed for days. The fire destroyed warehouses and factories along the riverbank. Finally the embarrassed community of Cleveland decided to clean up the Cuyahoga.

What stopped the polluting of the Cuyahoga River?

  Factries dumped chemikals into the river. This industreal waist combined with litter, and the hole river caught fire. The fire distroyed wherehouses and embarassed the city's recidents.

Lesson 25 is a test lesson. There is no worksheet.

Name _____

A _____

_____

B _____

_____

C As you know, many words in English came first from Greek, then Latin, then French and finally came into English. For many of these words, the spelling changed each time the word went into a new language.

Some words did not follow these steps. Instead they went from Latin directly into English. Here's why they didn't go from Latin to French and then to English:

Two thousand years ago, a great Roman general named Julius Caesar led an army that invaded England. The Roman invaders spoke Latin. The English used some Latin words to communicate with the invaders. These words went directly from Latin into English.

For hundreds of years, people who were well educated learned to read Latin. Some Latin words became part of the English language.

Below are some words that went directly from Latin into English. Notice that the spellings changed.

Latin	English
tributum	tribute
milites (soldiers)	military, militant
discipulus	disciple
credo	creed
victoria	victory
fortuna	fortune
planta	plant

Write the answers to the items.

1. Many words in English came from Greek, then Latin, then French. Did the word **fortune** follow these steps? How did the Romans spell the word **fortune?**

   _____

2. Why did people who spoke English 2,000 years ago learn some Latin words?

   _____

Use English words from the list to complete each item.

3. The entire school was excited about the team's _____ .

4. His success was due to good _____ .

5. The Garden Shop sells hundreds of _____ .

6. The word **discipline** is related to the word _____ .

D Five of these words are misspelled. Find the misspelled words. Then write them correctly.

1. importance
2. acommodate
3. beautiful
4. desaster   _____
5. thorough
                     _____
6. omit
7. refrase   _____
8. embarrassed   _____
9. consistent   _____
10. ocur
11. indurance
12. casually

52   Lesson 26

E
Write the morphographs for each word. Figure out any morphographs you don't know. Use Word Parts.

1. _____ + _____ = military
2. dis + _____ + _____ = discipline
3. _____ + _____ = begin
4. _____ + ate + _____ = duration

END OF LESSON 26

27 Name _____

A

B Write the word for each meaning clue.

origin   disaster   graphic   invisible   astronomer   advise

1. a drawing _____
2. where something comes from _____
3. can't be seen _____
4. a scientist who can name the stars _____
5. a terrible event _____
6. to help someone solve a problem _____

C Circle the misspelled word in each group. Then write it correctly.

1. medicine
   prehaps
   acknowledge
   valuable
   _____

2. shopper
   athletically
   intrest
   separate
   _____

3. suported
   usage
   autobiography
   easier
   _____

4. admirable
   information
   pulsate
   mistriel
   _____

5. performance
   confusion
   flatten
   freindliness
   _____

6. imaginary
   plesure
   basic
   service
   _____

Lesson 27

D Add the morphographs together. Remember to use your spelling rules. <u>W</u> at the end of a morphograph is a vowel letter.

1. trans + fer = _____
2. know + ledge = _____
3. pro + pel = _____
4. al + lot + ment = _____
5. com + mit + ment = _____
6. grow + th = _____
7. hap + y + est = _____
8. vise + ual = _____
9. al + low + ed = _____
10. industry + al = _____

END OF LESSON 27

A

B

1. pro + pel + ing   = _____
2. ad + mit + ance   = _____
3. com + mit + ment   = _____
4. re + cur + ing   = _____
5. trans + fer + ed   = _____
6. cur + tail   = _____
7. al + lot + ed   = _____
8. ex + cel + ence   = _____
9. for + got + en   = _____
10. un + hap + y   = _____

C

When **ch** sounds like **k** in a word, it probably came from Greek. Here is why. The Greeks had two different sounds for **k.** One sounded like our **k** sound. The other Greek **k** sound sounded like a hoarse **k.** The Romans did not have a letter for this sound, so they used their letters **c** and **h** to write this sound: **ch.**

Here are some words that had this letter in Greek: **ch**emical, s**ch**ool, me**ch**anic, and stoma**ch.**

People often misspell words that have this **ch** spelling for the **k** sound. Here are some words that are often misspelled: psy**ch**ology, **ch**aracter, heada**ch**e, melan**ch**oly, me**ch**anics, te**ch**nique.

Write the answers to the items.

1. How many **k** sounds did the Greeks have? _____

2. How do you know the word **scheme** comes from Greek? _____

3. Does the word **change** come from Greek? _____
   How do you know?

4. Does the word **echo** come from Greek? _____
   How do you know?

5. Two Roman letters aren't pronounced in the _____
   word **psychology.** Which letters are they?

Add the morphographs together. Use your rules. All these words have the k sound spelled ch.

6. school + ing = _____

7. character + ist + ic = _____

8. head + ache = _____

9. mechan + ic + al = _____

10. cheme + ist + ry = _____

11. echo + es = _____

12. back + ache = _____

13. cheme + ic + al = _____

14. scheme + ate + ic = _____

15. anchor + ed = _____

16. melan + choly = _____

17. chore + us = _____

18. chord + s = _____

19. techno + loge + y = _____

Lesson 28

D Make 8 real words from the morphographs in the box.

| en | bid | for | sake | give | got |

1. _____ 5. _____

2. _____ 6. _____

3. _____ 7. _____

4. _____ 8. _____

E Write the morphographs for each word. Figure out any morphographs you don't know. Use Word Parts.

1. _____ + th + _____ = healthy

2. _____ + trol + _____ = controlled

3. _____ + _____ = safety

4. _____ + gin + _____ = beginning

END OF LESSON 28

58   Lesson 28

Name _____

A

1. _____
2. _____
   _____

B

1. o + mit + ed   = _____
2. oc + cur + ence   = _____
3. al + lot + ment   = _____
4. per + mit + ing   = _____
5. pro + pel + er   = _____
6. pre + fer + ed   = _____
7. com + mit + ee   = _____
8. per + hap + s   = _____
9. ex + cel + ed   = _____
10. un + con + trol + able = _____
11. re + pel + ent   = _____

C

Write the correct word for each sentence. If you are not sure of a word, look it up in the list of homonyms in the back of your workbook.

1. Please come **hear/here**. _____
2. The book has a **plain/plane** cover. _____
3. **Their/They're** answers were all **right/write**. _____
4. Our house is for **sail/sale**. _____

Lesson 29

D Five words are misspelled. Find the misspelled words. Then write them correctly.

1. confuseing
2. consistent
3. transfir
4. skeme
5. fantazy
6. knowledge
7. industrial
8. safety
9. excelent

E Add the morphographs together. Remember to use your spelling rules.

1. character + ist + ic = _____
2. image + ine + ary = _____
3. mechan + ism = _____
4. cheme + ic + al = _____
5. marry + age = _____
6. mode + est + y = _____
7. lone + ly + ness = _____
8. be + gin + er = _____

F In Lesson 31 you'll have a spelling contest. Some of the words below will be used in the contest.

physical	current	permission	character	carriage
physicist	poison	inform	philosophy	improvement
athlete	usual	modern	endurance	appearance

Lesson 30 is a test lesson. There is no worksheet.

Name _____ **31**

A

personal   personnel   questionable   questionnaire   personify   personality

B

1. _____
2. _____

C

English borrowed many words from French. Sometimes we used the French spelling. Other times we changed the spelling. Hundreds of years ago, the French word **personne** was taken over by the English. In England its spelling was changed to **person.** The morphograph **person** can be found in many words like **person**ify, **person**al, and **person**ality. Later, English borrowed another word from French: **personnel.** The word **personnel** means "a group of workers." The English word **personnel** was not built on the English morphograph **person;** it was borrowed directly from French and has kept the French spelling. This is why **personnel** is not like all the other words with **person. Personnel** has the French spelling with two **n**'s.

The French word **questionne** had a similar history. When we borrowed it, we changed the spelling to **question** and built many common words with it, like **question**able and un**question**ing. Much later, we borrowed the word **questionnaire.** We took the word **questionnaire** directly from the French instead of building a new word from our word **question.** So **questionnaire** has kept the original French spelling with two **n**'s.

Here are some regular English words. Write the morphographs for each word.

1. _____ + _____ + _____ = impersonal
2. quest + _____ = question
3. _____ + _____ + _____ = impersonate
4. _____ + _____ + _____ = personalize
5. _____ + _____ = personify
6. _____ + _____ + _____ + _____ = unquestionable
7. _____ + _____ + ity = personality

Lesson 31   61

Write the answer for each item.

8. Why is **personnel** spelled with two **n**'s? _____

9. Is the word **personal** based on French or English spelling? _____

10. Is **person** a short **cvc** morphograph? So in the word **person + ify,** does the **n** double? _____

D Find the misspelled words in the sentences. Then write the words correctly.

1. Only very important people were admited. _____
2. His autobiagraphy is excellent. _____
3. They misplased their bagage at the airport. _____
4. It was definitly a joyus ocasion. _____

E Four words in this exercise have the morphograph <u>duce</u> or the morphograph <u>duct</u>. In Latin <u>duce</u> and <u>duct</u> mean "to lead." Something that is conducted is led together. Add the morphographs together.

1. pro + duct + ion = _____
2. dis + ciple + ine + ary = _____
3. re + duce + ed = _____
4. re + cur + ent = _____
5. con + duct + or = _____
6. sur + round + ing = _____
7. re + bel + ion = _____
8. busy + ness + es = _____
9. dure + ing = _____
10. e + duce + ate = _____

END OF LESSON 31

Name _____ 32

A

On that site, she received a citation.

B

1. _____
2. _____

C Find the misspelled words in the student's answer. Then write the words correctly. Do not use Word Parts for this part.

Years ago, a group of farmers in central California decided that they had a coyote problem. They trapped, shot, and poisoned the coyotes until almost none remained. With all the coyotes gone, the number of mice skyrocketed until there were over 80,000 per acre. The mice overran the land, destroying millions of dollars worth of crops. Now the farmers really had a problem!

Why did the farmers decide to stop killing coyotes?

    The farmers probibly desided to stop traping and poizoning the coyotes because the coyotes are helpfull in killing the mice. The mice are a reel problem now, and the farmers wish the coyotes were back.

_____

_____

_____

_____

_____

_____

Lesson 32   63

D

Write the correct spelling for each word in the word column. Then write O, A, B, or C after each number in the rule column:

Write **O** if the word is spelled by just putting the morphographs together.
Write **A** if the final-**e** rule explains why the spelling is changed.
Write **B** if the doubling rule explains why the spelling is changed.
Write **C** if the **y**-to-**i** rule explains why the spelling is changed.

	rule		word
1.	_____ mechan + ism	=	_____
2.	_____ oc + cur + ed	=	_____
3.	_____ family + ar	=	_____
4.	_____ con + trol + ing	=	_____
5.	_____ re + com + mend + ed	=	_____
6.	_____ probe + able	=	_____
7.	_____ re + ceive + er	=	_____
8.	_____ manu + script	=	_____

E

The Greeks used **y** as a vowel more than we do. The Greeks had many words with **y** between two consonants. Some words borrowed from Greek are still spelled this way. In fact, most of our words that have **y** between two consonants came from Greek. The **y** in these words is a vowel letter. Here are some of those words: s**y**mbol, c**y**cle, m**y**stery, ps**y**chology, anal**y**sis, h**y**steria, rh**y**thm, ph**y**sical, paral**y**zed, s**y**non**y**mous, t**y**rant, h**y**pocrite, h**y**phen, ox**y**gen, h**y**pnosis, h**y**mn, h**y**drant.

Answer the items.

1. How do you know the word **hymn** comes from Greek?

   _____

2. Does the word **symbol** come from Greek? How do you know?

   _____

Lesson 32

Add the morphographs together.

3. myst + ic + al = _____

4. syn + onym = _____

5. physic + ian = _____

6. syn + onym + ous = _____

7. hymn + al = _____

8. hyphen + ate + ed = _____

9. symbol + ic = _____

10. myst + er + y + ous = _____

11. bi + cycle = _____

12. rhythm + ic + al = _____

13. an + onym + ous = _____

14. hyster + ic + al = _____

END OF LESSON 32

33 Name _____

A

1. _____   4. _____
2. _____   5. _____
3. _____   6. _____

B Circle the misspelled word in each group. Then write it correctly.

1. present
   exercise
   lengthy
   misterious
   _____

2. embarrass
   approach
   thoughtfull
   personnel
   _____

3. wonderful
   actually
   durring
   echo
   _____

4. intermission
   personality
   questionned
   symbolic
   _____

5. excellance
   computer
   enlighten
   autograph
   _____

6. manufacture
   inconsistent
   surround
   advize
   _____

C Write the morphographs for each word.

1. _____ + _____ + _____ = disappoint
2. _____ + onym = synonym
3. _____ + _____ = magician
4. _____ + _____ = fourth
5. _____ + _____ + _____ = unforgettable
6. _____ + _____ + _____ = regrettable

66 Lesson 33

D The morphograph **dict** means "speak" or "speech." Here are some words that use the morphograph **dict**.

dictate: You dictate when you give instructions out loud.

predict: The morphograph **pre** means "before." You predict something when you tell about it before it happens.

diction: The way you use words is your diction.

contradict: The morphograph **contra** means "opposite." When you say the opposite of what someone else has said, you contradict that person.

Write the morphographs for each word.

1. _____ + _____ = diction
2. _____ + _____ + _____ = prediction
3. _____ + _____ = contradict
4. _____ + _____ + _____ = dictation

Answer the items.

5. What does the morphograph **contra** mean? _____

6. What does the morphograph **pre** mean? _____

Write the correct words that contain <u>dict</u>.

7. The way she uses words is impressive. I wish I had her _____ .

8. I went to a friend who said he could _____ where I would be next week.

9. Fred always thinks the opposite of his sister. That's why he often _____ the things she says.

10. Mr. Martinez said, "Write **Part B** on your paper. I'm going to _____ some spelling words to you."

11. Some people can _____ the weather just by looking at the clouds.

END OF LESSON 33

34 Name _____

A

indict   edict   malediction   benediction

B

_____

C

1. _____

2. _____

D Find the misspelled words in these sentences. Then write the words correctly.

1. They aproached the campground with happyness.   _____
2. Some poisenous animals were in the area.   _____
3. They were not permited to camp near the lake.   _____
4. My philosephy is actally very realistic.   _____
5. Four road hazzards led to much confuseion.   _____

Lesson 34

E Make 10 real words from the morphographs in the box.

| cur | oc | ence | s | re | ed | con |

1. _____
2. _____
3. _____
4. _____
5. _____
6. _____
7. _____
8. _____
9. _____
10. _____

F In Lesson 33 you learned that the morphograph **dict** means "speech" or "speak." Here are other words that contain **dict**.

benediction: A benediction is speaking well of or a blessing.

malediction: A malediction is speaking badly about or a curse.

dictionary: A dictionary is an alphabetical listing of words with their pronunciations and meanings.

dictator: A dictator is a person who tells others what to do or has absolute power.

edict: An edict is an order or command.

indict: To indict is to charge with a crime in a court of law.

Write the morphographs for each word.

1. _____ + _____ = predict

2. _____ + _____ + _____ = dictator

3. _____ + _____ + _____ = malediction

4. _____ + _____ + _____ = dictionary

5. _____ + _____ = edict

6. _____ + _____ + _____ = contradiction

7. _____ + _____ + _____ = indictment

8. _____ + _____ + _____ = benediction

Write the correct words that contain the morphograph dict.

9. When I don't know the meaning of a word, I use the _____ .

10. The captain runs his ship as if he were a _____ .

11. The speaker closed the service with a _____ .

12. The peasants were unhappy when they learned about the king's newest _____ .

13. First he said one thing; then he said the opposite. He always _____ himself.

14. After studying the evidence for several weeks, the city attorney _____ two city officials.

Lesson 35 is a test lesson. There is no worksheet.

Name _____

A

1. _____
   _____
2. _____
3. _____
4. _____

B

The morphograph **sum** means "the highest or topmost." When Greeks and Romans counted or worked addition problems, they didn't start at the top and write their answer at the bottom. They started at the bottom and worked upwards, writing the total at the top. They called the total the sum because it was the topmost number.

When you give a **summary,** you tell a condensed version of something larger. You tell only about things of the highest importance.

The word **summit** means "the top or highest part." The summit of a mountain is the top of the mountain.

Write the morphographs for each word.

1. _____ + ar + _____ = summary
2. _____ + it = summit
3. _____ + _____ + _____ = summarize
4. _____ + _____ = sums
5. ____ + ____ + ____ + ____ + ____ = summarization
6. _____ + ate + _____ = summation
7. _____ + _____ = summed

Lesson 36   71

C Write the word for each meaning clue.

| dictionary | consent | support | dictate |
| personnel | indict | contradict | absent |

1. a group of workers _____
2. hold something up _____
3. when you are not here _____
4. a book for finding word meanings _____
5. say the opposite of what someone else has said _____
6. feel that something is all right _____
7. say words for someone to write _____
8. when the court tells you that you have done something against the law _____

D Write the morphographs for each word.

1. _____ + _____ + _____ = indictment
2. _____ + _____ + _____ = separate
3. _____ + _____ = symbolic
4. _____ + er + _____ = mystery
5. _____ + _____ + _____ + _____ = discoveries
6. _____ + _____ + _____ + _____ = characterization
7. _____ + _____ + _____ = synonymous
8. _____ + _____ + _____ = transferred
9. _____ + _____ + _____ = deceived
10. _____ + _____ = perceive

END OF LESSON 36

Name _____ **37**

A

1. _____   11. _____
2. _____   12. _____
3. _____   13. _____
4. _____   14. _____
5. _____   15. _____
6. _____   16. _____
7. _____   17. _____
8. _____   18. _____
9. _____   19. _____
10. _____   20. _____

B

The morphograph for the number **4** is usually **four.** This morphograph is used in **fourteen** and other words. Another morphograph is used for **4** in the words **forty** and **forties.**

Here are words with the morphographs **for** and **four.** Notice that you use a hyphen in words like **forty-one.**

forty	forties	four	four hundred two
fortieth	two hundred forty	ninety-four	fourteenth
forty-one	nineteen forties	fourth	three hundred thirty-four

Write these numbers below. Then write the word for each number.

Example: 40s = forties

400 = _____   94th = _____

140 = _____   40th = _____

14   = _____   4th = _____

Lesson 37

Write the morphographs for these words. Some morphographs are given.

1. _____ + th = fourth
2. _____ + _____ = fourteen
3. _____ + ty = forty
4. _____ + _____ + es = forties
5. _____ + _____ + _____ = fourteenth
6. _____ + _____ + eth = fortieth

C Write the correct spelling for each word in the word column.
Then write **0**, **A**, **B**, or **C** after each number in the rule column:

Write **0** if the word is spelled by just putting the morphographs together.
Write **A** if the final-**e** rule explains why the spelling is changed.
Write **B** if the doubling rule explains why the spelling is changed.
Write **C** if the **y**-to-**i** rule explains why the spelling is changed.

	rule		word
1.	_____	early + er =	_____
2.	_____	re + ject + ion =	_____
3.	_____	re + bel + s =	_____
4.	_____	ac + know + ledge + ed =	_____
5.	_____	be + gin + ing =	_____
6.	_____	sum + ar + ize =	_____
7.	_____	com + pel + ed =	_____
8.	_____	pre + dict + able =	_____

D We're going to treat **i-t-y** as one morphograph even though it's actually two morphographs. **Ity** is made by combining **i-t-e** plus **y** or combining **i-t** plus **y**. In either case, we end up with **i-t-y**. So we'll just treat **ity** as if it is one morphograph.

Add the morphographs together.

1. person + al + ity = _____

2. com + mode + ity = _____

3. dense + ity = _____

4. op + port + une + ity = _____

END OF LESSON 37

38   Name _____

A

There was a large hole in the beam, which made the bridge weak.

B

1. _____
2. _____

C

Sometimes words that are related have morphographs that have slightly different spellings. The morphographs **four** and **for** are called **allomorphs**. Another pair of allomorphs is **scribe** and **script**. The morphograph **scribe** means "to write," and it is used in these words: de**scribe**, in**scribe**. The words de**script**ion, in**script**ion, and **script**ure also contain a morphograph that means "to write." The morphograph is **script**.

Sometimes an allomorph makes a word easier to pronounce. The word **prescription** is much easier to pronounce than it would be with the allomorph **scribe**.

Write the morphographs for each word.

1. _____ + _____ = subscribe
2. _____ + _____ + _____ = subscription
3. _____ + _____ + _____ + _____ = indescribable
4. _____ + _____ = manuscript
5. _____ + _____ = prescribe
6. _____ + _____ + _____ = prescription

Answer the items.

7. What do you call morphographs that have the same meaning but slightly different spellings? _____

8. Look at these words: **admission/admit, permissible/permit, submissive/submit.** Write the allomorph for **miss**. _____

9. Write the allomorph for **scribe**. _____

Lesson 38

D Write the morphographs for each word.

1. _____ + _____ + _____ = recommend
2. _____ + _____ = various
3. _____ + nox = equinox
4. _____ + _____ + _____ = fortieth
5. _____ + _____ + _____ = activity
6. _____ + _____ = summed
7. _____ + vale + _____ = equivalent
8. _____ + _____ + _____ = preferring

E Add <u>ance</u> and <u>ing</u> to the words in the box to make 12 real words. Use your spelling rules.

| admit | perform | endure | vary | import | appear |

1. _____
2. _____
3. _____
4. _____
5. _____
6. _____
7. _____
8. _____
9. _____
10. _____
11. _____
12. _____

END OF LESSON 38

Lesson 38

Name _____

A

find   fury   create   close   story   list

B

1. _____   4. _____
2. _____   5. _____
3. _____   6. _____

C For words that have the morphograph **ceive,** there are related words that have the allomorph **cept.** When the **ceive** word ends in **ion** or **ive,** the allomorph **cept** is used.

Here are words that have the allomorph **ceive:**
conceivable   deceive   perceive   misconceive   receive

Here are related words that end in **ion** or **ive:**
conception   deceptive   perception   misconception   receptive

For each word with ceive, write a real word that ends with ion or ive.

1. misconceive _____
2. receive _____
3. perceive _____
4. preconceived _____
5. deceive _____

Lesson 39

D A student wrote this report. The report contains nine misspelled words. Write each of those words correctly.

Elephants are dissappearing rapidly. Unfortunetly, people kill them for there ivory tusks. Ivory is valueable not only because it is beutiful, but because it is used as a currancy like gold and silver coins in some countries. Its really regretable that these wonderfull creatures are being killed.

E Write the correct spelling for each word in the word column. Then write O, A, B, or C after each number in the rule column:

Write **O** if the word is spelled by just putting the morphographs together.
Write **A** if the final-**e** rule explains why the spelling is changed.
Write **B** if the doubling rule explains why the spelling is changed.
Write **C** if the **y**-to-**i** rule explains why the spelling is changed.

rule   word

1. _____ sum + ar + y   = _____
2. _____ ex + pense + ive   = _____
3. _____ year + ly   = _____
4. _____ for + ty + es   = _____
5. _____ re + gret + ful   = _____
6. _____ in + quire + y   = _____
7. _____ in + form + ate + ive = _____
8. _____ un + en + light + en + ed = _____

Lesson 40 is a test lesson. There is no worksheet.

41 Name _____

A
1. _____
2. _____
   _____
3. _____

B
_____
_____

C
You learned that <u>cept</u> and <u>ceive</u> are allomorphs. Each word below has a morphograph missing. Use either <u>ceive</u> or <u>cept</u> to complete each word. Write the entire words. Use your rules.

1. re _____ ion
2. incon _____ able
3. de _____
4. miscon _____ ion
5. de _____ ive
6. per _____ ed

D Add the morphographs together.

1. ex + cess + ive = _____
2. early + est = _____
3. create + ed = _____
4. create + ion = _____
5. fury + ous = _____
6. con + verse + ate + ion = _____
7. story + es = _____
8. rain + ing = _____

E The English language got its alphabet letters from the Romans. The word for **alphabet** comes from the Greeks. Many words used to describe grammar come from the Romans and Greeks. All of these words came from Greek or Latin: **paragraph, sentence, summary,** and **grammar.**

The word **punctuation** comes from Latin. **Punctu** means "point." All the points, or marks you use in writing, are called **punctuation marks.**

All of these words come from Latin: **punctuation mark, question mark, exclamation mark,** and **quotation mark.**

All of these words come from Greek first and then from Latin: **period, comma, asterisk,** and **apostrophe.**

For each punctuation mark, the name of the punctuation mark is given. Write the morphographs that make up the name. You can use Word Parts.

1. " quotation mark = _____ + _____ + _____ mark
2. ? question mark = _____ + _____ mark
3. * asterisk = _____ + isk
4. ; semicolon = _____ + _____

Answer the items.

5. What letters tell you that **hyphen** came from Greek? _____
   What letters tell you that **apostrophe** came from Greek? _____

6. What are the morphographs in **punctuate**? _____

7. What is the first morphograph in **quotation**? _____

8. The word **exclamation** is related to the word **exclaim.** _____
   What are the morphographs in **exclaim**?

9. The morphograph **semi** means "half" or "almost." _____
   A **semicolon** is almost a **colon.** What word means **half circle?**

END OF LESSON 41

Lesson 41

A

1. _____
2. _____
3. _____
4. _____

B Write answers for each item.

1. What do you call morphographs that have the same meaning but slightly different spellings? _____

2. Why is **personnel** spelled with two **n**'s? _____

3. Is an astrologer a scientist? Is an astronomer a scientist? _____

4. Write the allomorph of **four**. _____

5. How do you know that the word **scheme** comes from Greek? _____

6. How do you know that the word **hyphen** comes from Greek? (There are two clues.) _____

7. What does the morphograph **in** mean in the word **invisible**? _____

C

Make 9 real words from the morphographs in the box.

| de | scribe | script | ceive | ive | cept | per | ion | pre |

1. _____
2. _____
3. _____
4. _____
5. _____
6. _____
7. _____
8. _____
9. _____

D

As you know, a final silent **e** drops when you add a morphograph beginning with a vowel letter. You may have wondered why so many words end with a silent **e**. Here are two reasons:

In many words, the final **e** tells the readers to say the name of a vowel letter in the word. The **e** at the end of **hope** tells us to say the name of the letter **o** when we read that word. The **e** makes sure that you say the word differently from **hop**. The **e** at the end of **pine** makes that word different from **pin**.

Sometimes a final **e** tells us how to say a consonant letter in the word. The letter **c** can be pronounced like a **k** (as in pi**c**nic) or like an **s** (as in pla**c**e). Whenever a **c** is followed by an **e**, you say the **s** sound. Other reasons for a final silent **e** will be given in later lessons.

1. Circle the word in which you would hear the name of a letter.

    gath   gathe

2. These words confuse many people. Circle the two words in which you hear the name of a letter.

    breath   breathe   clothe   cloth

3. Circle the words from this list that have a letter **c** with the sound of **s**.

    trace   vice   pick   race   juice   police

    track   arc   voice   panic   nice   ace

END OF LESSON 42

43

Name _____

A

1. _____   11. _____
2. _____   12. _____
3. _____   13. _____
4. _____   14. _____
5. _____   15. _____
6. _____   16. _____
7. _____   17. _____
8. _____   18. _____
9. _____   19. _____
10. _____   20. _____

B   Find the misspelled words in the student's answer. Then write those words correctly.

The city of Perth is the capital of Western Australia. The most important feature of Perth's geography is the beautiful Swan River. Many parks and gardens are located throughout the city and along the river. The weather is usually sunny and warm. People who live in Perth enjoy the opportunity to take part in outdoor sports and hobbies such as tennis and photography. Visitors to the city do not feel like strangers for long because the people who live there are so friendly.

Why is Perth an ideal city for people who love the outdoors?   _____

    Perth has good whether so peeple who love the outdoors can spend a lot of time in the sun. They can viset gardens and parks or walk along the Swan River. People who like photografy can take many pictures of the river and other things. All these oppertunities make Perth an ideel city for people who like to do things outdoors.

_____

_____

_____

_____

_____

Lesson 43

C

Write the correct spelling for each word in the word column.
Then write O, A, B, or C after each number in the rule column:

Write **O** if the word is spelled by just putting the morphographs together.
Write **A** if the final-**e** rule explains why the spelling is changed.
Write **B** if the doubling rule explains why the spelling is changed.
Write **C** if the **y**-to-**i** rule explains why the spelling is changed.

	rule		word
1.	_____	re + fuse + al =	_____
2.	_____	in + fury + ate =	_____
3.	_____	create + ure =	_____
4.	_____	re + fer + ing =	_____
5.	_____	in + volve + ment =	_____
6.	_____	myst + er + y + ous + ly =	_____
7.	_____	simple + y =	_____
8.	_____	re + marry + ed =	_____

D

Write the morphographs for each word.

1. _____ + _____ + _____ = dictation
2. _____ + _____ + _____ + _____ = observation
3. _____ + _____ + _____ + _____ = conversation
4. _____ + _____ + _____ + _____ = presentation
5. _____ + s = clothes
6. _____ + _____ + _____ = enclosure

END OF LESSON 43

44 Name _____

A

proceed   procedure   precede   precedent   antecedent

B

1. _____
2. _____
3. _____
4. _____

C

Some of the most frequently misspelled words have the allomorphs **cede** or **ceed**. Although the allomorphs are spelled two different ways, they have the same meanings: "to move" or "to yield."

If you remember some facts about **cede** and **ceed**, you will never misspell words like con**cede**, pro**ceed**, or inter**cede**.

The allomorph spelled **ceed** takes only three prefixes. These are **pro**, **ex**, and **suc**. For all other prefixes use the allomorph spelled **cede**. (There is only one exception to these facts. The word **procedure** is spelled with only one **e**, but other words that begin with **proceed** are spelled with two **e**'s, like **proceeding** and **proceeded**.)

Choose cede or ceed, and then add the morphographs together.

1. suc + cede/ceed   = _____
2. re + cede/ceed   = _____
3. ex + cede/ceed + ed   = _____
4. pro + cede/ceed   = _____
5. pre + cede/ceed + ence   = _____
6. ante + cede/ceed + ent   = _____

Four words are misspelled. Write those words correctly.

7. succeding   12. recede
8. exceeds   13. precedent
9. interceeded   14. conceed
10. proceeded   15. antecedent
11. procedure   16. preceed

_____
_____
_____
_____

D   A student wrote this story. Seven words are misspelled. Write each of those words correctly.

My freind created a monster. The creture was six feat tall and wieghed a lot. The creature ate all the houses on our street. My friend was very woried, and her parents were furyous. The monster was very espensive to make, but my friend had to give it away.

_____
_____
_____
_____
_____
_____
_____

E   The morphograph <u>pre</u> means "before." The morphograph <u>pre</u> is a prefix because it comes before other morphographs. Four words in this exercise have the prefix <u>pre</u>. Add the morphographs together.

1. pre + dict + able   = _____
2. breath + less + ness   = _____
3. ad + mit + ing   = _____
4. heal + th + y + er   = _____
5. pre + sent + ate + ion = _____
6. pre + view + ing   = _____
7. in + dis + pense + able = _____
8. pre + pare + ed   = _____

Lesson 45 is a test lesson. There is no worksheet.

46 Name _____

A

1. _____
2. _____
   _____
3. _____
   _____

B The Greeks have a letter for **r** called **rho.** The Greeks make a mark by the letter **rho** in some words to tell the speaker to pronounce the **r** with an **h** sound. When Romans borrowed words from Greek, they spelled these words with the letters **rh.**

We still have their strange spelling in some words: **rh**ythm, **rh**ubarb, **rh**apsody.

The morphograph **rhino** means "nose." The morphograph **ceros** means "horn." A rhinoceros is an animal with a horn on its nose.

The word **rhyme** used to be spelled **rime.** But people thought **rime** must be a misspelling. They thought **rime** should be spelled like **rhythm,** so they changed the spelling to **rhyme.**

Add the morphographs together.

1. rhythm + ic = _____
2. rhetor + ic = _____
3. rheum + ate + ism = _____
4. rhino + ceros = _____
5. rhyme + ing = _____

Answer the items.

6. What are the different spellings for the **r** sounds in **rhinoceros?** _____
7. What are the different spellings for the **r** sounds in **rhubarb?** _____
8. **Rhino** is a shorter word for which animal? _____

9. The morphograph **rrhea** means "to flow." **Rhinorrhea** is a medical term for a very runny ▓ .

10. The word **rhythm** comes from Greek. How do you know? (There are 2 clues.)

11. The word **rhyme** does not come from Greek. Why is it spelled with **rh?**

C Write the morphographs for each word.

1. _____ + _____ = furious
2. _____ + _____ + _____ = transmitting
3. _____ + _____ = transit
4. _____ + _____ = summit

D

You have learned a rule about using the allomorphs **cede** and **ceed**. **Ceed** follows the prefixes **pro, ex,** and **suc**. All other prefixes take **cede**. The only exception is the word **procedure**.

Choose <u>ceed</u> or <u>cede</u>, and then add the morphographs together.

1. ante + cede/ceed + ent = _____
2. suc + cede/ceed + ed = _____
3. ex + cede/ceed + ing + ly = _____
4. re + cede/ceed + ing = _____
5. pre + cede/ceed + ed = _____
6. pro + cede/ceed + ing + s = _____
7. con + cede/ceed + s = _____
8. pro + cede/ceed + ure = _____

END OF LESSON 46

A

Circle the misspelled word in each group. Then write it correctly.

1. duration	2. repellent	3. committment	4. dictionary
aproach	rephrased	summary	breathless
visible	imagenary	succeeded	compelled
military	wonderful	rebellion	exercize

_____   _____   _____   _____

B

The English word **sentence** means "a group of words that begin with a capital letter and end with an ending mark." The Romans had a different meaning for this word. **Sentence** comes from the morphograph **sent** that means "to feel." This was the meaning used in Latin. In Latin, a sentence was an opinion or a feeling that somebody had. A sentence could be a story, a paragraph, or one line.

We still use the word **sentence** to mean "an opinion." If a court of law judges a person to be guilty of a crime, the person is **sentenced**. The **sentence** the person receives may be five years in prison, or it may be a month in jail.

Answer the items.

1. Write the morphographs in **sentence**.

2. What does the first morphograph in **sentence** mean?

3. What did the word **sentence** mean in Latin?

4. This item has an English meaning of **sentence**: She wrote a lovely **sentence**. What meaning of **sentence** is that?

5. This item has an English meaning of **sentence**: The judge will give her **sentence** tomorrow. What meaning of **sentence** is that?

C Add the morphographs together.

1. pre + cede + ent = _____
2. pre + script + ion = _____
3. re + serve + ate + ion = _____
4. rhyme + ed = _____
5. re + sent + ment = _____
6. pro + cede + ure = _____
7. scheme + ing = _____
8. pre + fer + ed = _____

D Write the answers for each item.

1. What are the different spellings for the **r** sounds in **rhinoceros**? _____

2. Write the allomorph for **cept**. _____

3. Write the two words in which you hear the name of a letter.
   breath   breathe
   clothe   cloth
   _____

4. The word **rhythm** comes from Greek. How do you know? (There are 2 clues.)
   _____
   _____

5. Which three prefixes take the allomorph **ceed**? _____

END OF LESSON 47

48 Name _____

A

1. _____
   _____

2. _____
   _____

B Make 12 real words from the morphographs in the box.

| con | pre | ed | ceed | ex | cede | suc | pro | ing |

1. _____   7. _____
2. _____   8. _____
3. _____   9. _____
4. _____   10. _____
5. _____   11. _____
6. _____   12. _____

C Write the morphographs for each word.

1. _____ + _____ = divide
2. _____ + _____ + _____ + _____ = individual
3. _____ + _____ = weighed
4. _____ + t = weight
5. _____ + _____ + _____ = meaningless
6. _____ + _____ = meant

Lesson 48

D The words listed below come from Greek. In each word there are two clues that tell you the word is of Greek origin. Underline the clues in each word.

For example, the word **physical** has **ph** and a **y** between two consonants. When you write **physical,** underline these clues: **ph y**sical.

Remember that **ph, rh, ch,** and **y** between two consonants can all be clues.

1. rhythm
2. phonograph
3. psychology
4. morphograph
5. hyphen
6. synonym
7. physicist
8. symphony

E **Find the misspelled words in these sentences. Then write the words correctly.**

1. Her describtion was very graphic. _____
2. Some spies work on hazerdous buziness. _____
3. The originel information was lost durring the disaster. _____
4. The author planed to revize the mannuscript. _____
5. We're hopping that she will succede. _____

END OF LESSON 48

Lesson 48 93

49 Name _____

A Circle the misspelled word in each group. Then write it correctly.

1. admit
   really
   controled
   misspelling

   _____

2. spelled
   studying
   allotted
   decieved

   _____

3. synonim
   proceeded
   enjoyable
   noisier

   _____

4. thoughtful
   buried
   perscription
   perceptive

   _____

5. telegraph
   exceedingly
   loneliness
   akquired

   _____

6. casual
   replied
   symbowl
   scheme

   _____

B Write the word for each meaning clue.

| weak | prefix | pear | citation | fourth | summit |

1. a ticket _____
2. 4th _____
3. a certain fruit _____
4. the highest part of a mountain _____
5. a morphograph that comes before other morphographs _____
6. not strong _____

Lesson 49

C Write the correct spelling for each word in the word column.
Then write <u>O</u>, <u>A</u>, <u>B</u>, or <u>C</u> after each number in the rule column:

Write **O** if the word is spelled by just putting the morphographs together.
Write **A** if the final-**e** rule explains why the spelling is changed.
Write **B** if the doubling rule explains why the spelling is changed.
Write **C** if the **y**-to-**i** rule explains why the spelling is changed.

rule   word

1. _____ op + pose + ite   = _____
2. _____ rhythm + ic + al   = _____
3. _____ sym + phone + y   = _____
4. _____ ex + er + cise + s   = _____
5. _____ o + miss + ion + s   = _____
6. _____ family + ar + ize   = _____
7. _____ re + mit + ance   = _____
8. _____ dict + ion + ary + es = _____
9. _____ heal + th + y + er   = _____
10. _____ sur + face + ed   = _____

Lesson 50 is a test lesson. There is no worksheet.

51

A Here is the final-vowel rule: **Drop the final vowel** from a morphograph when the next morphograph **begins with a vowel.**

Add the morphographs together.

1. manu + age = _____
2. sacri + ed = _____
3. sacri + fice = _____
4. equi + al = _____
5. symbol + ic = _____
6. punctu + ure = _____
7. mode + est = _____
8. manu + script = _____

B

The coarse clouds will affect the weather.

C Write the morphographs for each word.

1. _____ + _____ + _____ + _____ = individual
2. _____ + _____ + _____ + _____ = disciplinary
3. _____ + _____ + _____ = sentenced
4. _____ + _____ = business
5. e + _____ = event
6. _____ + _____ + _____ = eventual

D

The morphograph **fine (fin)** may refer to completing something or putting it inside boundaries. Here are some words that use the morphograph **fine (fin)**.

final: The final thing you do is the ending thing you do, or the last thing you do.

finish: When you finish something, you complete it.

confined: When something is confined, it is put inside boundaries.

define: When you define something, you use words to make meaning boundaries.

Write the morphographs for each word.

1. _____ + _____ + _____ = confined
2. _____ + _____ = finish
3. _____ + _____ + _____ = finally
4. _____ + _____ + _____ + _____ = undefined

Write the correct words containing the morphograph fine (fin).

5. I'm almost done with this book. Right now I'm on the _____ chapter.
6. I will probably _____ it within an hour.
7. During the day the dog was _____ to his crate.
8. He tried to _____ seven words.
9. She will try to _____ her report on time.

E

Write the correct word or words for each sentence.

1. He bought a **peace/piece** of cloth. _____
2. We'll **meat/meet hear/here** at noon. _____

END OF LESSON 51

52 Name _____

A
Here is the final-vowel rule: **Drop the final vowel** from a morphograph when the next morphograph **begins with a vowel**.

Add the morphographs together.

1. sta + ate   = _____
2. manu + age   = _____
3. manu + script = _____
4. press + ure   = _____
5. contra + dict = _____
6. equi + nox   = _____
7. contra + ary = _____
8. equi + ate   = _____

B

The coarse clouds will affect the weather.

C
Find the misspelled words in these sentences. Then write the words correctly.

1. The author wrote four imaginetive storys. _____
2. Chris suceeded in deceiving everyone. _____
3. The dizaster occured fourty minutes ago. _____
4. His question embarassed us. _____

D In Lesson 51 you learned that the morphograph **fine (fin)** refers to completing something or putting it inside boundaries. Here are some more words with the morphograph **fine (fin).**

finite: Something that is finite is within the boundaries of things we can count.

definite: If something is definite, its boundaries are very clear. It is not vague.

infinite: Things that are infinite are beyond the boundaries of things we can count. The number of stars is infinite, meaning we cannot count them all.

definition: You make a definition when you describe or explain something exactly.

People often misspell words like **definitely** because they don't know that the word is related to other words with the morphograph **fine (fin).** If you know that the word is made of **fine (fin) + ite,** you know it has to be spelled **definitely,** even though you don't hear the sounds the way you do in the word **finite.**

Write the morphographs for each word.

1. _____ + _____ = finite
2. _____ + _____ + _____ = definite
3. _____ + _____ + _____ = infinite
4. _____ + _____ + _____ + _____ = definition
5. _____ + _____ + _____ + _____ + _____ = indefinitely

Write the correct words containing fine (fin).

6. They want to go to Hawaii, but their plans are not yet _____ .

7. There seems to be an _____ number of stars. I can never count them all.

8. Whenever I invite him to a party, he always says, "Maybe," or "Perhaps." He never gives me a _____ answer.

9. The opposite of **infinite** is _____ .

10. If you don't know what a word means, a dictionary is a good place to look for its _____ .

END OF LESSON 52

53 Name _____

A

Here is the final-vowel rule: **Drop the final vowel** from a morphograph when the next morphograph **begins with a vowel.**

Add the morphographs together.

1. ob + via + ous = _____
2. sta + ate + ment = _____
3. manu + fact + ure = _____
4. con + sta + ant = _____
5. se + pare + ate = _____
6. sacri + lege + ious = _____
7. de + via + ate = _____
8. mis + manu + age = _____
9. ad + equi + ate = _____
10. contra + dict = _____

B

_____

C

1. _____   5. _____
2. _____   6. _____
3. _____   7. _____
4. _____   8. _____

Lesson 53

D Make 8 real words from the morphographs in the box.

| al | de | ite | fine | in | ly | ish |

1. _____
2. _____
3. _____
4. _____
5. _____
6. _____
7. _____
8. _____

E The letters **tw** are often used as a short form of the word **two.** Here are some words with **tw**: **tw**enty, **tw**ice, **tw**ilight, **tw**elve, **tw**in, and be**tw**een. You don't hear the sound "tw" in the word **two,** but you hear it in these other words.

Write the missing word for each sentence.

1. There are _____ months in a year.

2. The fighting _____ the two countries continued for years.

3. Two people who are born at the same time are called _____ .

4. She tried it once, but he tried it _____ .

5. She had trouble seeing things in the _____ .

6. When you do something twice, you do it _____ times.

7. Ten plus two is _____ . Ten times two is _____ .

Lesson 53   101

F Write the morphographs for each word.

1. _____ + _____ = surface
2. _____ + _____ = profess
3. _____ + mode + _____ = commodity
4. _____ + _____ + _____ = rephrased
5. _____ + _____ + _____ = opportune
6. _____ + _____ = compare

END OF LESSON 53

Name _____

54

A

1. _____
2. _____

B

1. equi + vale + ent = _____
2. sta + ate + ion = _____
3. contra + dict + ion = _____
4. pre + via + ous = _____
5. di + sta + ance = _____
6. en + dure + ance = _____
7. sacri + fice + ial = _____
8. manu + fact + ure = _____

Lesson 54

C
A student wrote this report. Ten words are misspelled. Write each of those words correctly.

Exercise is very important if you want to be healthy and phisically fit. Running and swimming are to good forms of exersise. For both sports, you have to learn to breath right. Excessive running, when you are not used to it, can hurt you. You must disipline yourself to run short distinces. Find a good book that discribes how to start runing. Make inquiryes among your friends who run. Then start running. You may get an occasional ache or pain, but if you do it right, the occurences of your pains will become fewer and fewer.

D
Write the word for each meaning clue.

| affect | twenty-two | coarse | definite | infinite | twice |

1. two times
2. rough and ragged
3. beyond the boundaries of things we can count
4. not vague
5. make it change
6. 22

104   Lesson 54

E

Manu and **mani** are allomorphs. The morphograph **manu** means "hand" in these words: **manu**script, **manu**al. The words **mani**cure, **mani**pulate, and **mani**fest contain the morphograph **mani**.

Write the morphographs for each word.

1. _____ + _____ = manual
2. _____ + pule + _____ = manipulate
3. _____ + _____ + ate + _____ = manifestation
4. _____ + _____ = manuscript
5. _____ + _____ = manicure
6. _____ + _____ + _____ = manufacture

Answer the items.

7. Look at these words: **sacrifice/sacrament**. _____
   Write the allomorph for **sacri**.

8. Write the allomorph for **manu**. _____

9. The morphograph **pedi** means "feet." _____
   When you have your fingernails shaped,
   you have a **manicure**. What word means
   having your toenails shaped?

Lesson 55 is a test lesson. There is no worksheet.

56 Name _____

A

1. _____
   _____
2. _____

B

1. sta + ate + ment = _____
2. via + duct = _____
3. fine + al = _____
4. equi + ate + ion = _____
5. con + cluse + ive = _____
6. pre + via + ous = _____
7. sta + able = _____
8. e + sta + able + ish = _____

C Write the morphographs for each word.

1. _____ + _____ + ious = sacrilegious
2. _____ + _____ = sacrament
3. _____ + _____ + _____ + _____ = conversation
4. _____ + _____ = manicure
5. _____ + _____ + _____ = reversal
6. _____ + _____ + _____ + _____ = manifestation

106   Lesson 56

D Most of the people in Australia, Canada, Great Britain, and the United States speak the same language—English. Although many English words are pronounced differently in these countries, most of the words are spelled the same. There are, however, some differences.

One man in the United States was almost entirely responsible for those differences. His name was Noah Webster. Webster started writing dictionaries about 200 years ago. He thought many English words were not spelled the way they sounded, so he changed the spellings. For example, Webster spelled the words **build** and **laugh** like this: **bild, laf.**

Most people did not like these new spellings, so they didn't use them. Some of Webster's spellings, however, became widely used in the United States and in parts of Canada. The lists show some of those words.

How the words are spelled in Australia, Great Britain, and parts of Canada:		**How the words are spelled in the United States and parts of Canada:**	
grey	tyre	gray	tire
mould	programme	mold	program
colour	plough	color	plow
favourite	humour	favorite	humor
centre	glamour	center	glamor

Use the words from the lists to complete the sentences below. Use the spelling that is most common where you live. If you are not sure which spelling to use, look up the word, or ask your teacher.

1. My grandfather's hair turned _____ when he was very young.
2. The only _____ my sister likes is blue.
3. In some parts of the world, farmers still use horses or oxen to _____ their fields.
4. Marie can cheer up anyone with her terrific sense of _____ .
5. My bicycle has a flat _____ .
6. Dessert is my _____ part of a meal.
7. Reading Mastery Transformations is the name of the _____ that this spelling exercise is part of.
8. Bob put flowers in the _____ of the table.

END OF LESSON 56

57

Name _____

A

1. patri + on = _____
2. sacri + fice = _____
3. manu + age = _____
4. tele + phone = _____
5. a + muse + ment = _____
6. equi + al + ly = _____
7. ob + via + ous + ly = _____
8. equi + di + sta + ant = _____

B

The principal gave me advice.

C

Write the correct spelling for each word in the word column. Then write 0, A, B, or C after each number in the rule column:

Write **0** if the word is spelled by just putting the morphographs together.
Write **A** if the final-vowel rule explains why the spelling is changed.
Write **B** if the doubling rule explains why the spelling is changed.
Write **C** if the **y**-to-**i** rule explains why the spelling is changed.

	rule		word
1.	_____	manu + age =	_____
2.	_____	verse + ion =	_____
3.	_____	manu + script =	_____
4.	_____	vary + able =	_____
5.	_____	in + sta + ant =	_____
6.	_____	en + dure + ance =	_____
7.	_____	sacra + ment =	_____
8.	_____	study + ed =	_____

D Find the misspelled words in the student's answer. Then write those words correctly.

Dolphins are excellent swimmers. They are also extraordinary leapers. One scientist wondered why they occasionally travel over the water in huge, ten-foot leaps, when they can swim through it with so little effort. Are they just having fun?

The scientist measured the size and weight of the dolphins, the speed at which they swim, and the distance they leap. He made an amazing discovery. By leaping out of the water, the dolphins were saving energy. The faster a dolphin tries to swim, the more work it has to do to get through the water. Once it reaches a certain speed, the dolphin can actually save energy by hurling itself into the air, which does not drag against the dolphin the way water does.

Why do dolphins leap?

    By taking measurements of speed, wait, and distence, a sientist found out how hard a dolphin works when it's swimming. His calclations showed that above a certian speed, it is easyer to jump into the air than travel thorough water. Leaping saves energy.

END OF LESSON 57

Lesson 57

58 Name _____

A
Write the correct spelling for each word in the word column.
Then write **0**, **A**, **B**, or **C** after each number in the rule column:

Write **0** if the word is spelled by just putting the morphographs together.
Write **A** if the final-vowel rule explains why the spelling is changed.
Write **B** if the doubling rule explains why the spelling is changed.
Write **C** if the **y**-to-**i** rule explains why the spelling is changed.

	rule			word
1.	_____	swim + er	=	_____
2.	_____	radio + ate	=	_____
3.	_____	patri + on + ize	=	_____
4.	_____	pro + pel + er	=	_____
5.	_____	equi + ate + or	=	_____
6.	_____	radio + loge + y	=	_____
7.	_____	in + fury + ate	=	_____
8.	_____	change + ing	=	_____

B
The principal gave me advice.

C
Here is the final-vowel rule: Drop the final vowel from a morphograph when the next morphograph begins with a vowel, unless you hear both vowel sounds.

1.	punctu + ate	=	_____
2.	patri + on	=	_____
3.	patri + ot	=	_____
4.	sta + able	=	_____
5.	radio + ant	=	_____
6.	manu + al	=	_____
7.	radio + act + ive	=	_____
8.	patri + arch	=	_____

D The morphograph **migra** means "to wander." Here are some words that use the morphograph **migra**.

migrate: Migrate means to move to a new location.

migrant: Something that is wandering is migrant. A person who wanders is a migrant.

emigrate: The morphograph **e** means "away or out." When you leave your country, you emigrate.

immigrate: The morphograph **im** means "in or into." When you immigrate, you come to a new home in a new country.

migratory: Animals that migrate are migratory animals.

Write the morphographs for each word.

1. _____ + _____ = migrate
2. _____ + _____ = migrant
3. _____ + _____ + _____ = immigrant
4. _____ + _____ + _____ = emigrant
5. _____ + _____ + _____ + _____ = immigration
6. _____ + _____ + ory = migratory

Write the answer for each item.

7. Why does **immigrate** have two **m**'s? _____
8. What does the morphograph **im** mean? _____
9. What does the morphograph **e** mean? _____

Write the correct words using migra.

10. The pilgrims _____ from Europe because they were not happy there.

11. Some birds _____ thousands of miles every year.

12. In 1788 the first European _____ came to Australia.

END OF LESSON 58

Lesson 58

59 Name

A

B
Here is the final-vowel rule: Drop the final vowel from a morphograph when the next morphograph begins with a vowel, unless you hear both vowel sounds.

1. vacu + ate = _____
2. e + vacu + ate = _____
3. muse + um = _____
4. im + migra + ant = _____
5. punctu + ure = _____
6. contra + ary = _____
7. punctu + al = _____
8. muse + ic = _____

C

1. _____

2. _____

Lesson 59

D You know that some words are spelled two different ways in different countries. For example, people in Australia and Great Britain use the spelling **colour.** People in the United States use the spelling **color.** Both spellings are used in Canada.

Circle the spelling that is more appropriate for where you live. If you are not sure which spelling to use, look up the word in a dictionary, or ask your teacher.

1. armor / armour
2. harbour / harbor
3. favour / favor
4. labor / labour
5. flavour / flavor
6. color / colour
7. vapor / vapour
8. honor / honour
9. neighbor / neighbour
10. behaviour / behavior
11. valour / valor
12. odor / odour
13. humor / humour
14. glamour / glamor

E Circle the misspelled word in each group. Then write it correctly.

1. patronage
   dictionary
   manicure
   imigrate
   _____

2. sacrifice
   infuriate
   misstake
   conscientious
   _____

3. permitted
   conceive
   radial
   instint
   _____

4. equator
   embarrass
   defenition
   sacrament
   _____

5. station
   referral
   twinty
   finally
   _____

6. glorious
   pleasure
   obviously
   equil
   _____

7. establish
   afect
   sacrilege
   confined
   _____

8. denial
   unfortunat
   health
   distance
   _____

Lesson 60 is a test lesson. There is no worksheet.

61 Name _____

A

1. _____

2. _____
   _____

B Add the morphographs together.

1. re + act + ion = _____

2. sta + ate + ion = _____

3. coarse + ly = _____

4. de + part + ment + al = _____

5. manu + age + er + ial = _____

6. radio + ate + ion = _____

7. manu + fact + ure = _____

8. equi + vale + ence = _____

9. a + muse + ment = _____

10. ob + via + ous + ly = _____

C

**Write the correct spelling for each word in the word column.
Then write O, A, B, or C after each number in the rule column:**

Write **O** if the word is spelled by just putting the morphographs together.
Write **A** if the final-vowel rule explains why the spelling is changed.
Write **B** if the doubling rule explains why the spelling is changed.
Write **C** if the y-to-i rule explains why the spelling is changed.

	rule		word
1.	_____	trans + fer + ed =	_____
2.	_____	clear + ance =	_____
3.	_____	muse + um =	_____
4.	_____	muse + ic + ian =	_____
5.	_____	di + sta + ance =	_____
6.	_____	weigh + t =	_____
7.	_____	carry + ing =	_____
8.	_____	vacu + ant =	_____

D

Write the correct word or words for each sentence.

1. They have been married for **to/two** years. _____
2. Kim can fly a **plain/plane**. _____
3. Jesse gathered **wood/would** for the fire. _____
4. The **meat/meet** was on **sail/sale**. _____

END OF LESSON 61

62 Name

A

1. _____
2. _____
3. _____
4. _____
5. _____
6. _____
7. _____
8. _____
9. _____
10. _____
11. _____
12. _____
13. _____

14. _____
15. _____
16. _____
17. _____
18. _____
19. _____
20. _____
21. _____
22. _____
23. _____
24. _____
25. _____

B
Write morphographs for each word. Put a + between the morphographs.

1. reporter = _____
2. clearance = _____
3. recommended = _____
4. evacuate = _____
5. amusement = _____
6. sacrilege = _____
7. exceedingly = _____
8. excessively = _____

C
Find the misspelled words in these sentences. Then write the words correctly.

1. The creature was raydioactive.   _____
2. The preformance was amuzing.   _____
3. We approached the barial cite at twilight.   _____

Lesson 62

D The morphograph **ify** means "to make." Here are some words with the morphograph **ify**.

simplify: When you make something simpler, you simplify it.

classify: When you put things into groups or classes, you classify them.

falsify: When you make something false or lie about it, you falsify that thing.

justify: When you give reasons why your actions are right, you justify your actions.

Write the morphographs for each word.

1. _____ + _____ = falsify
2. _____ + _____ + _____ = classified
3. _____ + _____ + _____ = simplifying
4. _____ + _____ + _____ + _____ = unjustifiable

Write the correct words with the morphograph ify.

5. This explanation is too hard for me to understand. Can you _____ it for me?

6. He always tries to _____ his actions so they seem reasonable.

7. Some people _____ food into four groups: meat, dairy products, fruits-vegetables, and cereals.

8. People who _____ their records could face jail time.

For each word below make up a word that ends in ify. Example: notice – notify.

9. identity _____
10. signal _____
11. intensive _____
12. mode _____
13. horrible _____

END OF LESSON 62

Name _____

63

A

Stationery is on sale in aisle two.

B **Add the morphographs together. Remember to use your spelling rules.**

1. sta + ate + ment = _____
2. ex + pedi + ent = _____
3. origin + al = _____
4. equi + ate + ion = _____
5. pedi + al = _____
6. re + e + sta + able + ish = _____
7. simple + ice + ity = _____
8. simple + ify + ed = _____

C **A student wrote this report. Nine words are misspelled. Write each of those words correctly.**

When we went to the museum Sunday, we discoverred that it was closed. There was a notice on the door from the management. The notise said that the managment regretted imforming its partrins that the muzeum wood be closed indefinately. Before it could be reopened, certain repairs had to be made on the building.

We were very disapointed.

_____
_____
_____
_____
_____
_____
_____
_____
_____

Lesson 63   119

D For each word below make up a word that ends in <u>ify</u>. Example: <u>glorious – glorify</u>.

1. quality _____

2. terrible _____

3. identical _____

4. mystical _____

E You have learned the word **malediction** and what it means. A **malediction** is "speaking badly about, or a curse." The part of **malediction** that you know is **dict**. That part means "speech or speak." The part that you don't know is **male**. You know that **malediction** is "something that is very bad or evil." So you may be able to figure out that **male (mal)** means "evil or harmful." Below are some words that use the morphograph **male**.

malice: We say that an evil person is full of malice. An evil person is malicious.

malady: Malady is another word for sickness or a harmful disease.

malignant: When something is malignant, it is very harmful or dangerous.

Write morphographs for each word.

1. _____ + _____ = malice
2. _____ + _____ + ious = malicious
3. _____ + ade + _____ = malady
4. _____ + ign + _____ = malignant

Write the correct words with <u>male</u>.

5. We were so relieved when the doctor told us Mother did not have a _____ growth.

6. She is very sick now, but she hasn't had that _____ for very long.

7. He did so many evil things that we knew he was a _____ person.

8. Although her life has been very rough, she is not full of _____ .

END OF LESSON 63

Name _____

64

A

benign   beneficial   benevolent   malice   malicious

B

Stationery is on sale in aisle two.

C

1. _____
2. _____

D Write the morphographs for each word. Put a + between the morphographs.

1. original   _____
2. submit   _____
3. museum   _____
4. vacuum   _____
5. malice   _____
6. malicious   _____
7. station   _____
8. nutrient   _____

Lesson 64

E. You have learned that **male** means "bad or evil." The opposite of **male** is **bene**. You already know that a **benediction** is speaking well of or a blessing. Below are some words that use the morphograph **bene**.

benevolent: A benevolent person is a good or kind person.

benefit: Something that benefits you is good for you.

benefactor: A benefactor is a person who is good to other people or who benefits them.

benign: If something is benign, it is not harmful. If a diseased part is benign, it is not malignant. It will not harm you.

beneficial: Something that is beneficial for you is good for you.

Write the morphographs for each word.

1. _____ + _____ = benefit
2. _____ + vole + _____ = benevolent
3. _____ + _____ = benign
4. _____ + _____ + _____ = benefactor
5. _____ + fice + _____ = beneficial
6. _____ + _____ + _____ = benediction

Write the correct words with bene.

7. The growth on Mother's leg is not malignant. It is _____ .

8. A lot of sleep is _____ for babies.

9. My aunt is so helpful and kind. She is the most _____ person I know.

10. Sandra hopes that her experiences abroad will really _____ her.

11. His father is very kind to many people. Those people call him a _____ .

Lesson 65 is a test lesson. There is no worksheet.

Name _____

A

_____

B

1. _____
2. _____

_____

C A frequently misspelled word is **sandwich.** The spelling of the word is easier if you know the word's origin. The word **sandwich** came from someone's name, so **sandwich** is a single-morphograph word. The man was an Englishman named John Montague. He was the **Earl of Sandwich.** The earl loved to play cards and play pool. He was so involved with his games that he would sometimes go for more than a day without stopping to sleep. He was too impatient to sit down for a meal, so he invented the sandwich. He did this by putting a piece of meat between two slices of bread. He did not need a knife and fork to eat it.

Answer the items.

1. Who invented the **sandwich?** _____

2. Some people spell **sandwich** this way: **sandwitch.** They do this because they think **sandwich** has two morphographs. Which two morphographs do they think it has?

   _____

3. How many morphographs are in the word **sandwich?**

   _____

4. The word **sandal** is a single-morphograph word. It came from the Greek word for a wooden shoe—**sandalion.** Many people think **sandal** is made of two morphographs. If it were, what two morphographs would you use to make **sandal?**

   _____

Lesson 66

D Add the morphographs together.

1. peri + il = _____
2. nutri + ite + ion = _____
3. e + duce + ate = _____
4. spy + ed = _____
5. e + spy + on + age = _____
6. ex + pedi + ite = _____
7. ex + peri + ment = _____
8. de + via + ate + ion = _____

E Write the correct spelling for each word in the <u>word</u> column.
Then write <u>O</u>, <u>A</u>, <u>B</u>, or <u>C</u> after each number in the <u>rule</u> column:

Write **O** if the word is spelled by just putting the morphographs together.
Write **A** if the final-vowel rule explains why the spelling is changed.
Write **B** if the doubling rule explains why the spelling is changed.
Write **C** if the **y**-to-**i** rule explains why the spelling is changed.

rule   word

1. _____ bene + ign = _____
2. _____ im + pedi + ment = _____
3. _____ pedi + al = _____
4. _____ af + fect + ion = _____
5. _____ bene + fice + ial = _____
6. _____ of + fice + ial = _____
7. _____ class + ify + ing = _____
8. _____ non + com + mit + al = _____

END OF LESSON 66

Name _____ **67**

A

conscious   conscience   scientist   conscientious

B

1. _____
2. _____

C

spacious   nutritious   malicious   cautious   vicious

D

Write the correct spelling for each word in the **word** column.
Then write **O**, **A**, **B**, or **C** after each number in the **rule** column:

Write **O** if the word is spelled by just putting the morphographs together.
Write **A** if the final-vowel rule explains why the spelling is changed.
Write **B** if the doubling rule explains why the spelling is changed.
Write **C** if the **y**-to-**i** rule explains why the spelling is changed.

	rule		word
1.	_____ ident + ify + ed	=	_____
2.	_____ sandwich + es	=	_____
3.	_____ bene + fice + ial	=	_____
4.	_____ of + fice	=	_____
5.	_____ auto + bio + graph + ic + al	=	_____
6.	_____ pedi + al	=	_____
7.	_____ re + gret + able	=	_____
8.	_____ of + fice + ial	=	_____

Lesson 67   125

E Circle the misspelled word in each group. Then write it correctly.

1. manifested
   beneficial
   clasified
   spies
   _____

2. obvious
   impedament
   direction
   vacuum
   _____

3. deviate
   education
   benevolent
   maliss
   _____

4. experiment
   stationery
   equaly
   twenty-four
   _____

F You may have learned that **science** is a single-morphograph word. Actually, it is made up of two morphographs—**sci** plus **ence**. This passage tells more about the morphograph **sci**.

The morphograph **sci** means "to know." This morphograph is pronounced different ways, but it is always spelled the same way. And its spelling does not follow the final-vowel rule.

The morphograph **sci** is pronounced "sigh" in some words. In other words, it makes the sound "sh." In the words below, **sci** sounds like "sigh."

science: The organization of knowledge is called science.

scientist: Someone who has special knowledge or is looking for knowledge is called a scientist.

scientific: Something that is related to science is scientific.

In the words below, **sci** sounds like "sh."

conscious: If your mind is awake and you know what's going on around you, you are conscious.

conscience: Your conscience is the part of your mind that knows right from wrong.

conscientious: If you work hard, you are conscientious.

Regardless of the way **sci** is pronounced, the **i** in **sci** never drops. When we add **sci** to **ence**, the vowel does not drop. **Sci + ence** is spelled **science**. Remember, **sci** may be pronounced two ways, but the **i** never drops. If you remember that rule, you will be able to spell four of the most commonly misspelled words. They are **science, conscious, conscientious,** and **conscience.**

Write the morphographs for each word.

1. _____ + _____ + _____ = conscience

2. _____ + _____ + _____ + _____ = unconscious

3. _____ + _____ = science

4. _____ + _____ + _____ + _____ = conscientious

5. _____ + _____ + ist = scientist

Write the correct words containing sci.

6. Her _____ wouldn't let her steal the pie.

7. Biology and chemistry are branches of _____ .

8. A hard blow on his head knocked him _____ .

END OF LESSON 67

68 Name _____

A

conscientious   gracious   conscious   cautious   vicious

B

_____ _____ _____

C Make 8 real words from the morphographs in the box.

| migra | ate | radio | ant | vacu | ion | equi |

1. _____   5. _____
2. _____   6. _____
3. _____   7. _____
4. _____   8. _____

D

In words that come from Latin, the letters **q-u** act like two consonants, not like a consonant and a vowel. Words that come from Latin are easy to identify. The letters **q-u** make the sound "kw" in these words. Because the letters **q-u** stand for two consonant sounds, we treat **q-u** as two consonants. Remember that if the letters make the sound "kw," they are two consonants.

The **q-u** in the word **quit** makes the "kw" sound. So the word **quit** is a consonant, consonant, vowel, consonant. The word is a short word that ends **cvc**. Because **quit** ends **cvc**, the final consonant doubles in words like **quitter, quitting,** and **acquittal.** Remember that if the letters **q-u** are pronounced "kw," they are two consonants.

The underlined parts of the morphographs below end **cvc**:

quiz + ed = quizzed   e + quip + ed = equipped

Like most short morphographs that end **cvc,** the final **c** is doubled when the next morphograph begins with a **v.**

128   Lesson 68

1. Why does the **t** double in the word **quitter**?
   _____

2. Why doesn't the **r** double in the word **inquired**?
   _____

3. Why doesn't the **t** double in the word **quieter**?
   _____

4. Why does the **z** double in the word **quizzed**?
   _____

Combine the morphographs.

5. e + quip + ment = _____
6. quiz + ic + al = _____
7. quote + ed = _____
8. ac + quit + ed = _____
9. ac + quire + ed = _____
10. quit + ing = _____

E Write the answers for each item.

1. A **benevolent** person is a good or kind person. What is a **malevolent** person?   _____

2. What does the morphograph **bene** mean?   _____

3. Does the **i** ever drop from the morphograph **sci**?   _____

4. Who invented the **sandwich**?   _____

END OF LESSON 68

69 Name

A

verse   virtue   tract   fort

B

_____   _____   _____

C

strenuous   virtuous   vacuous   continuous   conspicuous

D

_____

_____

E Add the morphographs together.

1. space + ious = _____
2. grace + ious + ness = _____
3. dis + ap + pear + ance = _____
4. in + ex + peri + ence + ed = _____
5. com + pete = _____
6. com + pete + ite + ion = _____
7. com + pete + ite + or = _____
8. con + tinue + ous = _____

F Write the word for each meaning clue.

| conscience | beneficial | immigrant | conscious | sandwich |

1. someone who migrates into a country _____
2. when your mind is awake _____
3. a piece of meat between two slices of bread _____
4. something that is good for you _____
5. the part of your mind that knows right from wrong _____

G You learned that **q-u** pronounced "kw" works like two consonants. So a word like **quit** is actually a short morphograph that ends **cvc**.

Add the morphographs together. Remember that q-u acts like two consonants when it sounds like "kw."

1. quit + er = _____
2. e + quip + ment = _____
3. in + quire + y = _____
4. quiz + ed = _____
5. e + quip + ed = _____
6. ac + quit + al = _____
7. ac + quaint + ed = _____
8. quiet + ed = _____

Lesson 70 is a test lesson. There is no worksheet.

Lesson 69 131

71 Name _____

A

continu**ous**   conspic**uous**   virt**uous**   stren**uous**   ten**uous**

B

1. spac _____
2. conspic _____
3. virt _____
4. nutrit _____
5. grac _____
6. malic _____

C

_____
_____

D

1. _____
2. _____

E Write the morphographs for each word. Remember to put a + between them.

1. compete　　　_____
2. competition　_____
3. vacuous　　　_____
4. vacuum　　　_____
5. equipment　　_____
6. equipped　　　_____
7. comply　　　　_____
8. fortify　　　　_____

F Find the seven misspelled words in the student's answer. Then write the words correctly.

Sometimes two different animals cooperate in a way that benefits both of them. When they do, their relationship is called commensalism. The relationship between the rhinoceros and a bird called a tick bird is a good example of commensalism. The rhinoceros has many annoying parasites living in the folds of its skin. These insects are a fine source of food for the tick bird, which makes its home on the rhino's back. The bird gets all the food it wants, and the rhino gets rid of annoying pests. A tick bird often lives its entire life on a rhino's back.

Explain the arrangement between the rhinoceros and the tick bird.

　　The tick bird is a bird that lives on the back of a rhinoseros. This resorseful bird eats the annoying ensects it finds in the folds of the rino's skin.

　　This relationship benifits both the rhino and the tick bird. This arangement is called commensalism.

END OF LESSON 71

Lesson 71　133

72 Name _____

A

1. stren _____   3. contin _____   5. caut _____
2. grac _____   4. consc _____   6. cur _____

B

conquer   conquest   antique   acquaintance   quietly

C

_____
_____

D Make 9 real words from the morphographs in the box.

| quiz   quit   count   ac   ing   quire   ed |

1. _____   6. _____
2. _____   7. _____
3. _____   8. _____
4. _____   9. _____
5. _____

E Add the morphographs together.

1. multi + ply = _____
2. re + fuse + ed = _____
3. se + pare + ate + ion = _____
4. oc + cur + ed = _____
5. in + di + vide + ual = _____
6. ex + peri + ence = _____
7. e + vacu + ate = _____
8. ap + ply + ing = _____

F If words with **q-u** make the sound "kw," they are from Latin. If they do not make the sound "kw," but make a sound like "koo" or "kur," they are not Latin words.

Write all the Latin words. Do not write any words that are not from Latin.

| acquitted | conquest | acquaintance | inquiry |
| conquer | mosquito | quietly | |

_____ _____ _____

_____ _____

END OF LESSON 72

Name _____

A

1. virt _____
2. luxur _____
3. ten _____
4. spac _____
5. conscient _____
6. vic _____
7. conspic _____
8. caut _____

B

1. _____
2. _____
_____

C

Two words in this exercise have the morphograph **luxe**. The morphograph **luxe** means "fancy." Something that is deluxe is very fancy.

Add the morphographs together.

1. re + loco + ate = _____
2. suc + cess + ful = _____
3. loco + al = _____
4. ap + ply = _____
5. luxe + ury = _____
6. luxe + ury + ous = _____
7. ident + ify = _____
8. vice + ious + ness = _____

D You know that some words can be spelled two ways, depending on where you live. **Program** and **programme** are two spellings of one word. **Centre** and **center** are two spellings of another word.

Most longer words containing **program** or **programme** have only one spelling. **Programming** is a correct spelling everywhere in the English-speaking world. Here's why the spelling is the same whether we start with **program** or **programme**.

The doubling rule applies to **pro + gram + ing = programming**.

The final-vowel rule applies to **pro + gramme + ing = programming**.

Most words built from **centre** and **center** have only one spelling. The reason is that all English-speaking people use the allomorph **centre** to make longer words, like **central** and **concentrate**.

Add the morphographs together.

1. centre + al = _____

2. gramme + ar = _____

3. gram + ar = _____

4. con + centre + ate = _____

5. ec + centre + ic = _____

6. pro + gram + er = _____

7. pro + gramme + er = _____

8. de + centre + al + ize = _____

END OF LESSON 73

Lesson 73

74 Name _____

A

1. _____
2. _____
3. _____
4. _____
5. _____
6. _____
7. _____
8. _____
9. _____
10. _____
11. _____
12. _____
13. _____
14. _____
15. _____
16. _____
17. _____
18. _____
19. _____
20. _____
21. _____
22. _____
23. _____
24. _____
25. _____

B

1. _____
2. _____

C Write the correct spelling for each word in the word column.
Then write O, A, B, or C after each number in the rule column:

Write **O** if the word is spelled by just putting the morphographs together.
Write **A** if the final-vowel rule explains why the spelling is changed.
Write **B** if the doubling rule explains why the spelling is changed.
Write **C** if the y-to-i rule explains why the spelling is changed.

        rule   word

1. _____ un + pro + tect + ed = _____
2. _____ com + pel + ing = _____
3. _____ de + luxe = _____
4. _____ dis + loco + ate = _____
5. _____ un + con + trol + able = _____
6. _____ con + sci + ous = _____
7. _____ e + quip + ment = _____
8. _____ con + centre + ate = _____

D Three words in this exercise have the morphograph **tain**. In Latin **tain** means "to hold." A container holds things.

Add the morphographs together.

1. pro + fess + ion = _____
2. per + tain + ing = _____
3. centre + al = _____
4. enter + tain = _____
5. cure + ious = _____
6. pro + ject + ion = _____
7. main + tain = _____
8. re + ject + ed = _____

Lesson 75 is a test lesson. There is no worksheet.

Name _____

A

1. _____

2. _____

B

You know these words.   **These words sound the same.**

pear   pair: two
weight   wait: not doing something yet
waist   waste: things you throw away

Write the correct word for each sentence.

1. We bought apples and **pairs/pears**.   _____

2. That belt won't fit around his **waist/waste**.   _____

3. I'll **weight/wait** ten more minutes.   _____

4. The **weight/wait** of the snow made the roof fall in.   _____

5. Riki has a **pair/pear** of twin sisters.   _____

6. Busy people don't like to **waist/waste** time.   _____

C Write the morphographs for each word. Remember to put a + between them.

1. weighed _____
2. weight _____
3. profess _____
4. presentation _____
5. affectionate _____
6. wasteful _____
7. experimental _____
8. absent _____

D Find the misspelled words in these sentences. Then write the words correctly.

1. The experiment was a sucess. _____
2. We made to sandwitches. _____
3. They requirred more equipment. _____
4. Exercize can benifit your health. _____

END OF LESSON 76

77 Name _____

A

1. _____

2. _____

B Write the correct word or words for each sentence.

1. She lost **weight/wait** around her **waste/waist**.   _____
2. We have a peach tree and a **pair/pear** tree.   _____
3. Some people **waste/waist** money on luxuries.   _____
4. The train can't **weight/wait** any longer.   _____
5. Kim bought a **pear/pair** of tickets.   _____

C Write the morphographs for each word. Remember to put a + between them.

1. waiter _____
2. unsuccessful _____
3. manually _____
4. wholesome _____
5. excessive _____
6. science _____
7. multiply _____
8. previous _____

D Circle the misspelled word in each group. Then write it correctly.

1. identify
   pedel
   museum
   simplify
   _____

2. vacuum
   expedient
   sandwich
   dipartment
   _____

3. wieghed
   previous
   experience
   radiate
   _____

4. approach
   admire
   conshence
   luxury
   _____

5. perceive
   varyous
   pitying
   fortieth
   _____

6. equiped
   conquer
   acquittal
   quiz
   _____

7. conscious
   individuel
   manifest
   mystery
   _____

8. acquainted
   absent
   equal
   constent
   _____

E Write the word for each meaning clue.

competitors   simplify   deluxe   challenge   pair

1. have a contest with   _____
2. other contestants   _____
3. make simple   _____
4. fancy   _____
5. two   _____

END OF LESSON 77

78 Name _____

A

poison<u>ous</u>   fam<u>ous</u>   joy<u>ous</u>   nervous   tremendous

B Add the morphographs together.

1. loco + ate + ion = _____
2. ap + ply + ance = _____
3. story + es = _____
4. ply + able = _____
5. nerve + ous = _____
6. treme + or = _____
7. treme + end + ous = _____
8. ident + ify + ing = _____
9. leve + er = _____
10. e + leve + ate + ion = _____

C A student wrote this letter. Eight words are misspelled. Write each of these words correctly.

Dear David,

    Thank you for the lovely note you cent. I can't denie that I've weighted a long time to right you. I'm so absint-minded these days. I'm constintly forgeting things. In fact, I've forgotten why I'm writing you. My conscince has been telling me to write, so I have.

Love,

Sis

_____   _____   _____

144   Lesson 78

D Many words in the English language end in the allomorph **er**: swimm**er**, bowl**er**, farm**er**. The morphograph **er** means "one who." Here's a rule about most of those: they came after the shorter word. The word **swim** came before the word **swimmer**.

The word **beggar** is different. It is spelled differently because it came about differently. The word **beg** did not come into the language first. The word **beggar** came first. This word came from a group of monks called **beggards**. The monks asked people on the street for food. Their name was spelled **b-e-g-g-a-r-d,** so the word **beggar** is spelled with the letters **a-r,** not **e-r.** The word **beg** came into the language later. **Beg** told what beggars do. The word **beggar** is a single-morphograph word.

Answer the items.

1. What does the morphograph **er** mean?

   _____

2. By the spelling of these words you can tell which word probably came first. Circle the words that came first.

   box, boxer   receive, receiver

   photograph, photographer   writer, write

   voter, vote   manage, manager

3. What are the morphographs in **swimmer?**

   _____

4. A **beggar** is one who begs. If **a-r** were a morphograph in the word **beggar,** what would it mean?

   _____

5. **A-r** is not a morphograph in **beggar.** How many morphographs is **beggar?**

   _____

END OF LESSON 78

A

1. _____
2. _____

B

ridicul<u>ous</u>   synonym<u>ous</u>   numer<u>ous</u>   hazardous   famous

C

1. suspic _____
2. fam _____
3. consc _____
4. var _____
5. conspic _____
6. tremend _____
7. cur _____
8. contin _____

D Add the morphographs together.

1. ridicule + ed = _____
2. ridicule + ous = _____
3. com + ply + ance = _____
4. numer + ic + al = _____
5. numer + ous = _____
6. marry + age = _____
7. marry + ing = _____
8. re + leve + ant = _____
9. deny + al = _____
10. beauty + ful = _____

E Write the morphographs for each word. Remember to put a + between them. Two of these words are single-morphograph words.

1. performance _____
2. proceeded _____
3. conceivable _____
4. varying _____
5. beggar _____
6. classifying _____
7. forgotten _____
8. experience _____
9. sandwich _____
10. pliable _____

F In Lesson 81 you'll have a spelling contest. Some of the words below will be used in the contest.

equipped	resent	ridicule	creation
acquainted	luxury	pedal	disappoint
embarrass	advice	elevator	conquer

Lesson 80 is a test lesson. There is no worksheet.

81 Name ___

A
Write the correct spelling for each word in the **word** column.
Then write **O**, **A**, **B**, or **C** after each number in the **rule** column:

Write **O** if the word is spelled by just putting the morphographs together.
Write **A** if the final-vowel rule explains why the spelling is changed.
Write **B** if the doubling rule explains why the spelling is changed.
Write **C** if the **y**-to-**i** rule explains why the spelling is changed.

rule   word

1. _____   myst + er + y + ous   = _____

2. _____   ter + or   = _____

3. _____   ter + ify + ing   = _____

4. _____   ob + ject + ion + able   = _____

5. _____   im + ply + ing   = _____

6. _____   in + spect + ion   = _____

7. _____   in + spect + or   = _____

8. _____   hi + story   = _____

B
Write the correct word for each sentence.

1. We found a **pair/pear** of shoes.   _____

2. The table could not support the **wait/weight**.   _____

3. She doesn't want to **waist/waste** any more time.   _____

C Sometimes a longer word comes into the language first, and a shorter word comes later. An example is the word **beggar.** It is the longer word; it came first. The shorter word, **beg,** came later.

When the longer word comes first, we say the shorter word is a "back formation." Here's another example of back formation. The word **veterinarian** came into the language first. The word **vet** came later.

Answer the items.

1. The word **gymnasium** is a very old word. It comes from Greek. _____
What shorter word later came from **gymnasium?** Write it.

2. The word **caravan** is a very old word. It is a group of people and _____
their belongings that move like a train from place to place.
A shorter word has come from the word **caravan.** It refers
to something that moves from place to place. But this thing
is a modern vehicle with an engine. Can you name it?

3. The words **examine** and **examination** are very old words. _____
What shorter word means "an examination"?

END OF LESSON 81

Lesson 81   **149**

82 Name _____

A

1. _____   6. _____
2. _____   7. _____
3. _____   8. _____
4. _____   9. _____
5. _____   10. _____

B

1. _____
2. _____

C

1. _____
2. _____

D Five of these words are misspelled. Find the misspelled words. Then write them correctly.

1. wasteful   7. profession   _____
2. centril   8. obvius   _____
3. sandwich   9. synonim   _____
4. beggar   10. conquer   _____
5. luxury   11. varyous   _____
6. strenuus   12. clearance

Lesson 82

E Add the morphographs together.

1. hurry + ing = _____
2. friend + ly + ness = _____
3. com + pete + ite + ion = _____
4. com + pete + ent = _____
5. op + port + une + ity + es = _____
6. worry + ed = _____
7. rob + er + y + es = _____
8. un + deny + able = _____

F Answer the items.

1. The word **laboratory** is an old word. This word refers to a place where you can make a careful study of things and how they work. A three-letter word later came from the longer word. Write that word. _____

2. The word **influenza** is an old word that refers to a sickness. Influenza is a common sickness that many people seem to get at the same time. People have a fever; they cough, and they ache; their noses run. After a few days they get better, but this sickness may hang on for weeks. The word that you know for **influenza** came after the older word. The modern word is three letters long and begins with **f.** Write that word. _____

3. A **submarine** is a vehicle that can travel completely underwater. A shorter word came after that word. The shorter word refers to the same vehicle. Write that word. _____

END OF LESSON 82

A

You know these words.   **These words sound the same.**

coarse   course: a route or path you follow
affect   effect: an outcome
site   sight: seeing

Write the correct word for each sentence.

1. The president will decide our next **coarse/course** of action. _____

2. Looking directly into the sun can harm your **site/sight**. _____

3. His yelling has a bad **affect/effect** on everyone around him. _____

4. We will build our house on that **site/sight**. _____

5. The storm will **affect/effect** traffic. _____

6. The wool is very **coarse/course**. _____

B Add the morphographs together.

1. glory + ous = _____
2. ab + rupt + ly = _____
3. hi + story + an = _____
4. for + ty + eth = _____
5. con + tain + er = _____
6. cor + rupt + ion = _____
7. cor + rect + ly = _____
8. multi + ply + ing = _____
9. ter + ible = _____
10. enter + tain + ment = _____

C **Find the ten misspelled words in the student's answer. Then write them correctly.**

Chemicals that we use to control pests can affect other animals as well. Suppose a field is sprayed to kill insects. The mice that live in the field eat the plants that have been sprayed. After a few weeks, the mice will have eaten so much seed that they may contain a very high concentration of the spray chemical. When an eagle or a falcon eats one of these mice, the bird takes a large dose of the chemical. The bird may die or lay eggs with weak shells that could never hatch. In this way the poison becomes part of a natural food chain and affects every animal in the chain.

How might humans be affected by the poisons we use on pests?

    People who use poison to controll pests don't realize that these dangerous cemichals can effect all animals, including humans. Anemals who eat poizoned insects probably won't die, but they may get weeker and their babyes may die. The meet we eat is at the end of the food chain, so it has had a chance to build up large consentrations of dangrous poisons.

END OF LESSON 83

84 Name _____

A

1. _____   4. _____

2. _____   5. _____

3. _____   6. _____

B Write the correct word for each sentence.

1. I took my friend to the golf **coarse/course**.   _____

2. Oil spills can have a serious **affect/effect** on seagulls.   _____

3. This material is too **coarse/course** to wear next to my skin.   _____

4. Seeing his friends again will probably **affect/effect** him.   _____

5. The church was rebuilt on the same **sight/site**.   _____

6. I can't see him anymore; he's out of **site/sight**.   _____

Words that end in consonant-and-**y** follow the final-vowel rule. The word **worry** ends consonant-and-**y**. When we add **ing**, we hear the sound for the **y** and the sound for the **i**. So we keep the letters for both sounds: **worrying**.

The word **glory** ends consonant-and-**y**. When we add **ify**, we do not hear the sound for the **y** and the sound for the **i**. So we drop the **y**. It does not change to **i**. Here's how we spell the word: **glorify**.

Say the word you get by combining **very + ify**. Does **very** end consonant-and-**y**? Do you hear the sound for both the **y** and the **i** in the combined word?

Say the word you get by combining **agony + ize**. Do you hear the sound for both the **y** and the **i**?

Remember this about words that end consonant-and-**y**. In words like **worrying, applying, studying, terrifying,** and **certifying,** you can hear both vowels, so we keep the **y**.

In words like **applicant, certificate, categorize, pacifist, historic,** and **terrific,** you cannot hear both vowels, so we drop the **y**.

Add the morphographs together.

1. beauty + ify = _____
2. apply + ing = _____
3. apply + icant = _____
4. certify + icate = _____
5. terrify + ic = _____
6. agony + ize = _____
7. history + ic = _____
8. terrify + ing = _____

Lesson 84

D The morphograph **uni** means "one." Below are words that use the morphograph **uni**.

unite: When parts unite, they become one thing.

uniform: When individual people wear a uniform, they wear one outfit. Everybody wears the same thing.

union: A group of things that have become one is called a union.

unicycle: A unicycle is a vehicle with only one wheel.

Write the morphographs for each word.

1. _____ + _____ = uniform
2. _____ + ion = union
3. _____ + _____ = unicycle
4. _____ + ite = unite

Answer the item.

5. One vowel drops in the words **union** and **unite**. What vowel? _____

Write the correct words using uni.

6. All those players have the same _____ .
7. The army and the air force will _____ forces.
8. The _____ of the two forces will make our country unbeatable.
9. Tina can ride a bicycle, but she can't ride a _____ .

Lesson 85 is a test lesson. There is no worksheet.

Name _____

A

1. _____
2. _____
   _____

B

You learned about dropping the final **y** from words that end in consonant-and-**y**. You drop the **y** when you can't hear it.

Combine the parts.

1. very + ify = _____
2. spy + ing = _____
3. certify + icate = _____
4. deny + ing = _____
5. justify + ication = _____
6. comply + icate = _____
7. supply + ing = _____
8. marry + ing = _____
9. history + ic = _____
10. category + ize = _____

C In Lesson 84 you learned that **uni** means "one." Here are other words that have the morphograph **uni**.

unique: Something that is one of a kind is unique.

unit: Whatever you count as one is a unit.

universe: The one thing that is in every direction you turn is the universe. It is so large that it is made of everything we know, all the stars, the planets, the sun, Earth—everything.

unison: When people speak in unison, they say the same thing at the same time. They speak as one person.

Write the morphographs for each word.

1. _____ + ique + _____ = uniqueness
2. _____ + _____ = universe
3. _____ + it = unit
4. _____ + _____ = unison

Answer the items.

5. One vowel drops in the words **unique** and **unit.** What vowel? _____

6. The morphograph **corn** means "horn." What do the morphographs in the word **unicorn** mean? _____

Write the correct words using uni.

7. The reason their team plays so well is that they all work together like a _____.

8. Everybody sang "Happy Birthday" in _____.

9. He looked up at the stars and said, "What a huge _____."

158   Lesson 86

D Write the morphographs for each word.

1. disruptive _____
2. unaffected _____
3. affection _____
4. reunite _____
5. effective _____
6. effort _____
7. fortify _____
8. certify _____

END OF LESSON 86

87

Name _____

A

1. _____
2. _____
3. _____
4. _____
5. _____
6. _____
7. _____
8. _____
9. _____
10. _____

11. _____
12. _____
13. _____
14. _____
15. _____
16. _____
17. _____
18. _____
19. _____
20. _____

B

1. _____
   _____
2. _____

C You learned about dropping the final **y** from words that end in consonant-and-**y**. You drop the **y** when you can't hear it.

Combine the parts.

1. bury + ing = _____
2. category + ize = _____
3. glory + ify = _____
4. terrify + ing = _____
5. multiply + ication = _____
6. certify + ing = _____
7. certify + icate = _____
8. prehistory + ic = _____
9. pacify + ing = _____
10. pacify + ist = _____

D In Lessons 84 and 86, you learned that **uni** means "one." Here are other words that have the morphograph **uni**.

unify: Another way of saying that things unify is they unite or become one.

unity: Unity is another word for oneness.

unanimous: The morphograph **anima** means "spirit or life." When something is unanimous, everybody agrees. Everybody behaves as if they are one in spirit or belief.

Write the morphographs for each word.

1. _____ + ify = unify
2. _____ + _____ + ic + _____ + _____ = unification
3. _____ + anima + _____ = unanimous
4. _____ + ity = unity

Lesson 87   161

Write the correct words using uni.

5. They are going to _____ the schools into one school district.

6. Since the team began to play like one single person, the team has a lot of _____ .

7. The decision to continue was _____ .

Answer the items.

8. One vowel drops in the words **unite, unify, union, unit, unique,** and **unity.** What vowel?   _____

9. Two vowels drop in the word **unanimous.** Which vowels?   _____

10. Three vowels drop in the word **unification.** Which vowels?   _____

11. What does the morphograph **anima** mean?   _____

12. The word **animal** is frequently misspelled. You can see   _____
    the morphograph **anima** in the word **animal.**
    Combine the morphographs....**anima** + **al** = ▇▇▇ .

END OF LESSON 87

Name _____

A

1. _____   3. _____
2. _____   4. _____

B

1. ten _____   4. caut _____   7. suspic _____
2. prev _____   5. hazard _____   8. synonym _____
3. unanim _____   6. malic _____

C Find the misspelled words in these sentences. Then write the words correctly.

1. The beggor told numerrous tales. _____
2. Our acommodations were grasious and luxerious. _____
3. Each applycant recieved a questionaire. _____
4. The corupt rober did not have a guilty consciense. _____

D Add the morphographs together.

1. uni + verse + al = _____
2. re + verse + al = _____
3. verse + ate + ile = _____
4. poison + ous = _____
5. ter + or = _____
6. ridicule + ous = _____
7. verse + ate + ile + ity = _____

Lesson 88

E You have learned the word **unicycle** and what it means. A **unicycle** is a vehicle with only one wheel. The part of **unicycle** that you know is **uni**. That part means "one." The part that you don't know is **cycle**. You know that a unicycle has only one wheel. So you may be able to figure it out that **cycle** refers to something that goes around in a circle. Below are some words that use the morphograph **cycle**.

bicycle: The morphograph **bi** means "two." A bicycle is a vehicle with two wheels.

tricycle: The morphograph **tri** means "three." A tricycle is a vehicle with three wheels.

cyclone: A cyclone is a wind that goes around and around, like a wheel.

cyclic: Things that are cyclic follow the same pattern of a wheel that goes around and around. Cyclic things happen again and again.

bicyclist: The morphograph **ist** means "one who." A bicyclist is someone who rides a bicycle.

Write the morphographs for each word.

1. _____ + _____ = bicycle
2. _____ + one = cyclone
3. _____ + _____ = unicycle
4. _____ + _____ = tricycle
5. _____ + _____ = cyclic
6. _____ + _____ + _____ = bicyclist

Answer the items.

1. What does the morphograph **uni** mean? _____

2. What does the morphograph **bi** mean? _____

3. What does the morphograph **tri** mean? _____

4. How many angles does a **triangle** have? _____

5. Something that is **equilateral** has equal sides. _____
   If **lateral** refers to sides, what is the word for
   something that has two sides?

END OF LESSON 88

Name _____

89

A

1. _____ 5. _____

2. _____ 6. _____

3. _____ 7. _____

4. _____ 8. _____

B

1. _____

2. _____

3. _____

C Add the morphographs together.

1. caut + ion = _____

2. caut + ious = _____

3. ter + ify = _____

4. super + flu + ous = _____

5. uni + it = _____

6. in + flu + ence = _____

7. flu + id = _____

8. hi + story + ic + al = _____

Lesson 89 165

D A student wrote this report. Nine words are misspelled. Write each of those words correctly.

At the last union meeting, we unanimusly voted to strike for higher wages. The workars in the bycicle dipartment will go on strike first. The people in the stuffed animel department will go on strike next. Since we will be striking right before the holidays, this will undenyably hurt busness, and we might have a better chance of getting our wages increased.

The next unyon meating will be held after work on Tuesday, November 18.

_____

_____

_____

_____

_____

_____

_____

_____

_____

E Write the morphographs in each word.

1. experiment   _____
2. interruption _____
3. fortunate   _____
4. bicycle   _____
5. universe   _____
6. pleasant   _____
7. competent   _____
8. effortless   _____

Lesson 90 is a test lesson. There is no worksheet.

Name

A You learned about dropping the final **y**. The only time you would ever drop the final **y** is when the next morphograph begins with **i** and you hear only one vowel sound. If the word ends consonant-and-**y** and the next morphograph begins with any letter but **i**, you never drop the **y**. You change the **y** to **i**.

When we combine **carry + age,** we get **carriage.** We cannot hear a sound for both the **y** and the **a**. We don't drop the **y** because the next morphograph does not begin with **i**. We just change the **y** to **i**.

When we combine **bury + ed,** we get **buried.** We cannot hear a sound for the **y** and for the **e**. We don't drop the **y** because the next morphograph does not begin with **i**. We just change the **y** to **i**.

Add the morphographs together.

1. marry + age = _____
2. glory + ous = _____
3. glory + ify = _____
4. busy + ness = _____
5. study + es = _____
6. ap + ply + ic + ant = _____
7. ap + ply + ing = _____
8. hi + story + an = _____

Lesson 91

B

You know these words.   **These words sound the same.**

stationery   stationary: can't move
aisle   isle: island
principal   principle: rule

Write the correct word for each sentence.

1. The crew was shipwrecked on a desert **aisle/isle**. _____

2. The **principal/principle** gave a speech on the first day of school. _____

3. A horse stood **stationary/stationery** in the field, staring at the cowboy. _____

4. Our secretary has ordered more office **stationary/stationery**. _____

5. The bride looked radiant as she walked down the **aisle/isle**. _____

6. It is against his **principals/principles** to cheat people. _____

C Write the word for each meaning clue.

| unique | beggar | bicycle | unite | cyclic |

1. a person who asks for food   _____
2. become one thing   _____
3. when things happen again and again   _____
4. a vehicle with two wheels   _____
5. one of a kind   _____

D The allomorphs **judge** and **judice** mean "to judge." Here are some words that use the allomorphs **judge** and **judice**.

judicial: Something related to the courts or the law is judicial.

judicious: Someone who is wise (capable of good judgement) is judicious.

misjudge: When you make a bad estimate, you misjudge.

prejudge: When you judge something before you should, you prejudge it.

prejudice: An opinion formed without knowledge or reason is prejudice.

Note: In parts of the English-speaking world, **judge + ment** is spelled **judgement.** In the United States and parts of Canada, this word is often spelled **judgment.**

Write the morphographs for each word.

1. _____ + _____ + _____ = misjudged
2. _____ + _____ = prejudge
3. _____ + _____ = prejudice
4. _____ + ious = judicious
5. _____ + ial = judicial
6. _____ + _____ + _____ = prejudicial

Answer this item.

7. What is unusual about this spelling of **judge + ment = judgment**?
   _____

Write the correct words using judge or judice.

8. Only the most _____ men and women should be leaders.
9. A courtroom is where most _____ questions are answered.
10. A person with a strong _____ has a lot of hate.
11. I try not to _____ people I don't know very well.
12. We _____ how much cake to make for the party.

END OF LESSON 91

A

1. _____
2. _____

B

Write the correct spelling of each word in the <u>word</u> column.
Then write <u>O</u>, <u>A</u>, or <u>C</u> after each number in the <u>rule</u> column:

Write **O** if the word is spelled by just putting the morphographs together.
Write **A** if the final-vowel rule explains why the spelling is changed.
Write **C** if the **y**-to-**i** rule explains why the spelling is changed.

    rule   word

1. _____ very + ify = _____
2. _____ like + ly + hood = _____
3. _____ marry + age = _____
4. _____ com + ply + ing = _____
5. _____ deny + ed = _____
6. _____ just + ify + able = _____
7. _____ agony + ize = _____
8. _____ category + es = _____

C

Write the correct word for each sentence.

1. There were sales in every **aisle/isle**. _____
2. Statues are **stationary/stationery**. _____
3. Scientists must study the rules and **principals/principles** of physics. _____
4. For our vacation, we stayed on an **aisle/isle** in the South Pacific. _____
5. Mark was sent to the **principal/principle**. _____
6. I need to buy more **stationary/stationery**. _____

D Find the misspelled words in these sentences. Then write the words correctly.

1. He commited a terible crime. _____
2. The historean was very buzy. _____
3. All morphografs have meenings. _____
4. The magisian performed two uneque tricks. _____

E Add the morphographs together.

1. anima + al = _____
2. uni + anima + ous = _____
3. super + flu + ous = _____
4. judice + ious = _____
5. flu + ent + ly = _____
6. re + uni + ion = _____

F In the next lesson you'll have a spelling contest. The words below will be used in the contest.

animal	category	ridicule	influence
competent	versatile	identify	bicycle
carriage	caution	wasteful	business

END OF LESSON 92

93 Name _____

A

1. _____
2. _____

B Write the word for each meaning clue.

| effect | affect | waist | waste | aisle | isle |
| sight | site | pair | pear | weight | wait |

1. seeing _____
2. make it change _____
3. two _____
4. your midsection _____
5. measurement of heaviness _____
6. a row _____
7. an island _____
8. an outcome _____
9. a place _____
10. a certain fruit _____
11. not doing something yet _____
12. things you throw away _____

C

Write the correct spelling of each word in the word column.
Then write O, A, B, or C after each number in the rule column:

Write **O** if the word is spelled by just putting the morphographs together.
Write **A** if the final-vowel rule explains why the spelling is changed.
Write **B** if the doubling rule explains why the spelling is changed.
Write **C** if the **y**-to-**i** rule explains why the spelling is changed.

	rule		word
1.	_____	uni + anima + ous =	_____
2.	_____	marry + age =	_____
3.	_____	pre + caut + ion =	_____
4.	_____	patri + ot =	_____
5.	_____	re + spect + able =	_____
6.	_____	com + pany + es =	_____
7.	_____	ter + ible =	_____
8.	_____	sci + ent + ist =	_____
9.	_____	sign + ify + ic + ant =	_____
10.	_____	sci + ent + ify + ic =	_____

D

Make 12 real words from the morphographs in the box.

| ident | uni | ed | ify | just | cert | very | ic | ate | ion |

1. _____   7. _____
2. _____   8. _____
3. _____   9. _____
4. _____   10. _____
5. _____   11. _____
6. _____   12. _____

END OF LESSON 93

Lesson 93

Name _____

A

1. _____
2. _____
_____

B

1. _____   5. _____
2. _____   6. _____
3. _____   7. _____
4. _____   8. _____

C Add these morphographs together.

1. com + pense + ate = _____
2. ac + com + pany + ment = _____
3. in + sist + ent = _____
4. con + sist + ence + y = _____
5. part + ial = _____
6. in + flu + ent + ial = _____
7. sub + sta + ant + ial = _____
8. re + spect + able = _____

D The morphograph **anti** means "against or opposite." Here are some words that use the morphograph **anti**.

antibody: An antibody is a cell that fights against disease in your body.

antonym: The morphograph **onym** means "name or word." Antonyms are words with the opposite meaning. **Hot** and **cold** are antonyms.

antisocial: Someone who doesn't like to be with people is antisocial.

antagonize: When you put somebody in agony or make that person mad, you antagonize the person.

antiperspirant: Something that fights perspiration is an antiperspirant.

Write the morphographs for each word.

1. _____ + soci + _____ = antisocial
2. _____ + onym = antonym
3. _____ + _____ + _____ = antibodies
4. _____ + _____ + spire + _____ = antiperspirant
5. _____ + agony + _____ = antagonize

Answer the items.

6. It is easy to make words using **anti**. Make up a word that means "against pollution." Make up a word that means "against war."

7. What does the morphograph **onym** mean?

8. The word **anonymous** means "without a name." What does the morphograph **an** mean in the word **anonymous**?

9. One vowel drops in the word **antonym**. What vowel?

10. Two vowels drop in the word **antagonize**. Which vowels?

Write the correct words containing anti.

11. **Soft** and **easy** are both _____ of the word **hard**.

12. Many people have _____ that keep them well.

13. The hermit is so _____ that he won't even talk to people.

14. He is very malicious. He likes to _____ people.

Lesson 95 is a test lesson. There is no worksheet.

Name _____ **96**

A You know these words.   These words sound the same.

two   too: also
hole   whole: entire
weak   week: seven days

Write the correct word or words for each sentence.

1. Let Jim come **too/two**. _____
2. We worked all **weak/week** long. _____
3. She has **too/two** new puppies. _____
4. They buried the treasure in a **hole/whole** on the beach. _____
5. The girls ate **too/two hole/whole** pies. _____
6. His illness left him **weak/week** and shaky. _____

B Add the morphographs together.

1. spire + it + ual   = _____
2. per + sist + ent   = _____
3. in + spire + ate + ion   = _____
4. con + serve + ate + ion = _____
5. anti + onym   = _____
6. philo + soph + ic + al   = _____
7. in + sist + ed   = _____
8. origin + ate   = _____
9. in + spect + ion   = _____
10. enter + tain + ment   = _____

Lesson 96   177

C The morphograph **preci** means "price or value." This morphograph is always pronounced the same way, but its spelling works like the spelling of **sci**. The final vowel never drops. Below are some words that use the morphograph **preci**.

precious: Something very valuable is precious.

appreciate: When you recognize the value of something, you appreciate it.

depreciate: When the value of something decreases, it depreciates.

unappreciative: When you don't appreciate something, you are unappreciative.

Write the morphographs for each word.

1. _____ + _____ = precious

2. _____ + _____ + _____ = depreciate

3. _____ + _____ + _____ = appreciable

4. _____ + _____ + _____ = appreciate

5. ____ + ____ + ____ + ____ + ____ = unappreciative

Write the correct words using preci.

6. The _____ guest failed to thank his host for the excellent meal.

7. Some people don't _____ helpful criticism.

8. Diamonds and rubies are _____ stones.

9. If her house _____ any more, it will be completely worthless.

END OF LESSON 96

Name

A Write the correct word or words for each sentence.

1. There's a **hole/whole** in this wall **too/two**. _____

2. The mansion took up the **hole/whole** block. _____

3. My sister likes her coffee **weak/week**. _____

4. Jim will leave in a **weak/week** or **too/two**. _____

B If the morphograph <u>ex</u> is followed by a morphograph that begins with <u>s</u>, drop the <u>s</u>.

1. ex + sist = _____

2. ex + cept = _____

3. ex + spect = _____

4. ex + ceed = _____

5. ex + pense = _____

6. ex + cite = _____

7. ex + spire = _____

8. ex + cel + ent = _____

C You may have learned that **motor** is a single-morphograph word. Actually it is made up of two morphographs—**mote** plus **or**. This passage tells more about the morphograph **mote**.

The morphograph **mote** means "to move." Here are some words that use the morphograph **mote**.

demote: When you move something to a lower position, you demote it.

remote: Something that is far away is remote.

promote: When you move something to a higher position, you promote it.

motion: Motion means movement.

motive: The reason for doing something is the motive.

Write the morphographs for each word.

1. _____ + _____ = motion

2. _____ + _____ = motive

3. _____ + _____ + _____ = automotive

4. _____ + _____ + _____ = promotion

5. _____ + _____ + _____ = commotion

6. _____ + _____ = motor

Write the correct words containing mote.

7. The blender won't run because the _____ is broken.

8. Good workers are _____ .

9. The South Pole is the most _____ part of the world.

10. Hunger was the thief's _____ for stealing the bread.

11. The _____ of the waves sometimes makes people seasick.

Lesson 97

D Write the correct spelling for each word in the word column.
Then write **O**, **A**, **B**, or **C** after each number in the rule column.

Write **O** if the word is spelled by just putting the morphographs together.
Write **A** if the final-vowel rule explains why the spelling is changed.
Write **B** if the doubling rule explains why the spelling is changed.
Write **C** if the y-to-i rule explains why the spelling is changed.

	rule		word
1.	_____	category + ize =	_____
2.	_____	per + secu + ute =	_____
3.	_____	com + pany + es =	_____
4.	_____	con + secu + ute + ive =	_____
5.	_____	be + gin + er =	_____
6.	_____	sign + ify + ic + ant =	_____
7.	_____	cert + ain =	_____
8.	_____	anti + onym =	_____

END OF LESSON 97

A

If the morphograph ex is followed by a morphograph that begins with s, drop the s.

1. ex + ceed = _____
2. ex + spect = _____
3. ex + cite = _____
4. ex + port = _____
5. ex + sist + ence = _____
6. ex + peri + ment = _____
7. ex + secu + ute = _____
8. ex + cel + ence = _____

B

Write the correct spelling for each word in the word column.
Then write O, A, B, or C after each number in the rule column.

Write **O** if the word is spelled by just putting the morphographs together.
Write **A** if the final-vowel rule explains why the spelling is changed.
Write **B** if the doubling rule explains why the spelling is changed.
Write **C** if the y-to-i rule explains why the spelling is changed.

rule   word

1. _____ pro + mote + ion = _____
2. _____ judice + ial = _____
3. _____ pro + fess + ion + al = _____
4. _____ hi + story + ic = _____
5. _____ ex + cel + ent = _____
6. _____ preci + ous = _____

C

For many words that have morphographs ending in the sound **d**, there is an allomorph that has an **s**. When we add the morphograph **ive** or **ion**, we use the allomorph with the **s**.

Here are some of those words. The second column shows the allomorph that comes before **ive** or **ion**.

comprehend	com + **prehense** + ion	= comprehension
explode	ex + **plose** + ive	= explosive
divide	di + **vise** + ion	= division
defend	de + **fense** + ive	= defensive

For each word below, write a real word that ends with the morphograph <u>ive</u>.

1. decide _____
2. persuade _____
3. offend _____
4. exclude _____
5. apprehend _____
6. include _____
7. expend _____
8. respond _____

D

A student wrote this letter. Ten words are misspelled. Write each of those words correctly.

Dear John,

    I'm so exsighted that you're coming to vizit us. Imajine, in just two weaks you'll be hear! I really appresiate the efort you're taking to come here. It will be so enjoiable to have companie.

See you soon,

J. J.

PS How do you like my new stationary?

END OF LESSON 98

Lesson 98   183

A

1. _____
2. _____
3. _____
4. _____
5. _____
6. _____
7. _____
8. _____
9. _____
10. _____

11. _____
12. _____
13. _____
14. _____
15. _____
16. _____
17. _____
18. _____
19. _____
20. _____

B Add the morphographs together. Use your spelling rules.

1. ex + spire = _____
2. ex + pand = _____
3. ex + panse + ion = _____
4. ex + cluse + ive = _____
5. ex + peri + ence = _____
6. ex + spect + ate + ion = _____
7. ex + secu + ute + ion = _____
8. ex + cess + ive = _____

C You have learned that many morphographs ending in a **d** sound have allomorphs that have an **s.** When we add **ive** or **ion,** we use the allomorph with the **s.** For each word below, write a real word that ends with the morphograph **ion.**

1. divide _____
2. comprehend _____
3. conclude _____
4. suspend _____
5. extend _____
6. erode _____
7. provide _____
8. invade _____

D Write the word for each meaning clue.

> judicious   too   antonym   motion   precious   whole

1. entire _____
2. a word with the opposite meaning _____
3. capable of good judgment _____
4. movement _____
5. also _____
6. something very valuable _____

Lesson 100 is a test lesson. There is no worksheet.

101 Name _____

A

1. _____ 4. _____
2. _____ 5. _____
3. _____

B When a word ends in the letters **a-g-e** and the next morphograph is **ous**, that part is spelled **a-g-e-o-u-s**. The final **e** is not dropped because the pronunciation of the **g** does not change. Remember how to spell the part that sounds like "age-us": **a-g-e-o-u-s**.

Add ous to these words. Remember that if the word ends in a-g-e, keep the final e.

Example: **outrage + ous = outrageous**

1. courage + ous = _____
2. joy + ous = _____
3. mystery + ous = _____
4. advantage + ous = _____
5. ridicule + ous = _____
6. continue + ous = _____

C Make 7 real words from the morphographs in the box.

| in | ex | clude | con | spire | sist |

1. _____ 5. _____
2. _____ 6. _____
3. _____ 7. _____
4. _____

186 Lesson 101

D Some morphographs ending in the **f** sound are related to allomorphs that end in the **v** sound. By listening to the word, you can tell whether to use the allomorph with **f** or the allomorph with **v**.

Here are some words with allomorphs ending in the **f** sound.

grief	mischief	thief	fifty
relief	belief	twelfth	knife

Here are related words that end in the **v** sound.

grievance	mischievous	thievery	five
relieve	believe	twelve	knives

For each word below, write a word that has an f sound.

1. believe _____
2. mischievous _____
3. grieved _____
4. five _____
5. thieves _____
6. twelve _____
7. relieved _____
8. wives _____

E Find the misspelled words in the sentences. Then write the words correctly.

1. Studyng sience is not a waist of time. _____
2. The questionnair was devided into four categoreys. _____
3. She is an inflooential exsecutive. _____
4. The dizaster effected the hole state. _____

END OF LESSON 101

A

B

Some words end with **ible**. Other words end with **able**. You can't tell which ending is used by the way the word is pronounced, and there is no rule that holds for all words. But there are some rules that will help you in most cases.

The ending we add to **nonwords** is usually **ible**. There are some exceptions, but here are some examples of nonwords that take **ible**:

increde	+ ible = incredible	poss	+ ible = possible
audi	+ ible = audible	suscept	+ ible = susceptible
hor	+ ible = horrible	transmiss	+ ible = transmissible
ter	+ ible = terrible	vise	+ ible = visible

The ending we add to **most** words is spelled **a-b-l-e**. There are exceptions to this rule too. But here are some words that follow the rule:

work + able = workable	predict + able = predictable
admire + able = admirable	excite + able = excitable

Some words that take **able** end in **g-e** or **c-e**. The final **e** doesn't drop in these words because the pronunciation is the same when we add **able**. So the **g** or the **c** must be followed by **e**. Here are some of those words:

change + able = changeable	notice + able = noticeable
manage + able = manageable	trace + able = traceable

1. permiss + able/ible = _____
2. service + able/ible = _____
3. poss + able/ible = _____
4. conceive + able/ible = _____
5. knowledge + able/ible = _____
6. compate + able/ible = _____
7. charge + able/ible = _____
8. consider + able/ible = _____

C Add ous to these words. Remember that if the word ends in a-g-e, keep the final e.

1. mystery + ous = _____
2. outrage + ous = _____
3. nerve + ous = _____
4. poison + ous = _____
5. courage + ous = _____
6. synonym + ous = _____
7. luxury + ous = _____
8. advantage + ous = _____

D You have learned that some morphographs ending in the **f** sound have allomorphs that end in the **v** sound. By listening to the word, you can tell whether to use the allomorph with the **f** or with the **v**. For each word below, write a word that has a **v** sound.

1. relief _____
2. thief _____
3. belief _____
4. fifty _____
5. wolf _____
6. knife _____

END OF LESSON 102

Name

A

1. _____
2. _____

B

Write the correct spelling for each word in the word column.
Then write O, A, or D after each number in the rule column:

Write **O** if the word is spelled by just putting the morphographs together.
Write **A** if the final-vowel rule explains why the spelling is changed.
Write **D** if the **ex** rule explains why the spelling is changed.

rule · word

1. _____ ex + spire = _____
2. _____ ex + peri + ence = _____
3. _____ di + vide + er = _____
4. _____ ex + tract + ion = _____
5. _____ pre + judice = _____
6. _____ be + lieve + able = _____
7. _____ per + secu + ute = _____
8. _____ ex + sist + ence = _____

C For some words that have a morphograph with a long-vowel sound there are related words that have short-vowel morphographs. The short-vowel morphograph is used when the word ends in **ion**. You can hear the difference in the sound of these morphographs.

| explain | repeat | reveal | exclaim |
| explanation | repetition | revelation | exclamation |

For each word below, write a real word that ends with ion.

1. explain + ion = _____
2. reveal + ion = _____
3. exclaim + ion = _____
4. repeat + ion = _____

D You learned some general rules for using **able** and **ible**. The ending we add to words is usually **able**. The ending we add to nonwords is usually **ible**. Words that end **g-e** or **c-e** take **able** and do not drop the final **e**.

Write each word with the morphograph able or ible. Some morphographs have already been combined.

1. exchange + able/ible = _____
2. excite + able/ible = _____
3. suscept + able/ible = _____
4. poss + able/ible = _____
5. incrède + able/ible = _____
6. trace + able/ible = _____
7. audi + able/ible = _____
8. manage + able/ible = _____

END OF LESSON 103

Lesson 103 191

A Some words with more than one syllable end in the sound "eek." The ending of these words is spelled **i-q-u-e**. The reason is that we use the French spelling for these words, and the French spell "eek" with the letters **i-q-u-e**.

The word that sounds like "criteek" is spelled **c-r-i-t-i-q-u-e**, and the word that sounds like "misteek" is spelled **m-y-s-t-i-q-u-e**. Here are the rest of the "eek" words: tech**nique**, an**tique**, phys**ique**, un**ique**.

These words are among the words most frequently misspelled. They are less difficult to spell if you remember that "eek" is spelled **i-q-u-e**.

1. _____
2. _____
3. _____
4. _____
5. _____
6. _____

B You learned that some long-vowel morphographs have short-vowel allomorphs. The short-vowel allomorph is used when the word ends in **ion**.

For each word below, write a real word that ends in ion.

1. repeat + ion = _____
2. explain + ion = _____
3. reveal + ion = _____
4. proclaim + ion = _____

Lesson 104

C. You learned some general rules for using **able** and **ible**. The ending we add to words is usually **able**. The ending we add to nonwords is usually **ible**. Words that end **g-e** or **c-e** take **able** and do not drop the final **e**.

Add the morphographs together. Choose <u>able</u> or <u>ible</u>. Use your spelling rules.

1. re + gret + able/ible = _____

2. just + ify + able/ible = _____

3. vise + able/ible = _____

4. note + ice + able/ible = _____

5. know + ledge + able/ible = _____

6. per + miss + able/ible = _____

7. ter + able/ible = _____

8. be + lieve + able/ible = _____

D. **In Lesson 106 you'll have a spelling contest. Some of the words below will be used in the contest.**

explain	manageable	courage	outrageous
explanation	relief	mystique	physique
technique	belief	repetition	decision

Lesson 105 is a test lesson. There is no worksheet.

A

The morphograph **soci** means "companion or friend." The morphograph is pronounced two different ways. The **c** sound makes the sound "sss" in some words and the sound "sh" in other words.

The spelling of **soci** works like the spelling of **sci** and **preci**. The final vowel never drops. Below are some words with the morphograph **soci**.

social: Things that are social involve having companions or friends.

society: A group of people who live and work together is called a society.

sociable: Someone who makes friends easily is sociable.

associate: When you put two things together, you associate them. Many people associate the flu with winter weather.

dissociate: When you separate two things, you dissociate them. He has dissociated himself from that gang of hoodlums. This word should not be spelled **disassociate**.

Write the morphographs for each word.

1. _____ + _____ + _____ = antisocial
2. _____ + _____ + _____ + _____ = association
3. _____ + _____ + _____ = dissociate
4. _____ + ety + _____ = societies

Answer the items.

5. Why does the word **associate** have two **s**'s? _____

6. What word means the opposite of **associate**? _____

Write the correct words containing soci.

7. Birds don't usually _____ with cats.

8. The Native Americans had the first known _____ in North America.

9. That hermit is so _____ that he hasn't spoken to anyone in ten years.

10. Several women formed a _____ club.

Lesson 106

B You already learned about the Greek morphographs for star: **aster** and **astro.** These allomorphs are in the words **astrology** and **disaster.**

The Latin morphograph for star is **sider.** The Romans were superstitious like the Greeks. They thought stars were involved in thinking. The word **consider** contains the Latin morphograph **sider.**

The French changed the Latin morphograph **sider** into **sire.** The French thought the stars had something to do with wishing for things. The word **desire** contains the French morphograph **sire.**

Write the morphographs for each word.

1. _____ + _____ = desire
2. _____ + _____ = consider
3. _____ + _____ + _____ + _____ = inconsiderate
4. _____ + _____ + _____ = desirable
5. _____ + _____ + _____ + _____ = consideration
6. _____ + _____ + _____ = desirous
7. _____ + _____ + _____ + _____ = undesirable
8. _____ + _____ + _____ + _____ = considerably

Write one of these meanings for each underlined word in the sentences.

| ill-starred event | wishes | thinks about |

9. She <u>desires</u> to become famous. _____

10. An earthquake is a natural <u>disaster</u>. _____

11. Julie always <u>considers</u> all her choices before deciding. _____

Write whether each morphograph is Greek, Latin, or French.

12. sider _____   14. aster _____

13. sire _____

END OF LESSON 106

107 Name _____

A

1. _____
2. _____

B The morphograph **fer** is in many words. It presents spelling problems because the **r** doubles for some endings but does not double for others. There's a simple way to tell whether the **r** in **fer** doubles: If the morphograph **fer** is stressed, or said loudly when you say the word, the **r** doubles. If **fer** is not stressed, the **r** does not double.

In these words the morphograph **fer** is stressed: **refer, confer, prefer.**

In these words the morphograph **fer** is not stressed: **offer, suffer, differ.**

When we add endings to words like **refer** and **confer,** the stress may change. If **fer** is no longer stressed in these words, the **r** does not double. In these words **fer** is not stressed: **reference, conference, preferable.** The **r** is not doubled in these words.

In these words **fer** is stressed, so the **r** is doubled: **conferred, referred, preferring.**

When you're adding the endings to a word that has the morphograph **fer,** say the word. If you stress **fer,** double the **r.** If you don't stress **fer,** do not double the **r.**

C There are two allomorphs for **9.** One is spelled **nine.** That morphograph is used in words like **nineteen.** The other allomorph is spelled **nin.** It always comes before **th.** The morphograph **nine** is used in all other words.

Here are words with the morphographs **nine** and **nin:**

ninety-five	twenty-ninth
nineteenth	ninth
ninetieth	forty-ninth

Write the word for each number.

Example: **90s = nineties**

19 = _____   90th = _____

9th = _____   99th = _____

D Some words that end in the sound "ur" are spelled with the letters **o-r** in the United States and are spelled with an **o-u-r** ending in the United Kingdom, Australia, and parts of Canada.

The U.S. spellings are **humor** and **labor;** the spellings in the United Kingdom and Australia are **humour** and **labour.**

Canada uses both spellings. Some people use the **o-r** spelling; others use the **o-u-r** spelling.

When you add **ize, ous,** or **ate** to any of these words that end with the sound "ur," the spelling is the same in all English-speaking countries. **Humorous** and **elaborate** are not spelled with **o-u-r,** even in England and Australia.

Add the morphographs to these words. Spell each word correctly.

1. vapor/vapour + ize = _____
2. glamor/glamour + ous = _____
3. labour/labor + ate + ory = _____
4. de + odor/odour + ize = _____
5. rigour/rigor + ous = _____
6. glamor/glamour + ize = _____
7. e + vapor/vapour + ate = _____
8. humor/humour + ous = _____

END OF LESSON 107

108. Name _____

A Some college-level words end in the morphographs **ane + ous**. When these morphographs are combined, do not drop the final **e**. Remember that the combined part is always spelled **a-n-e-o-u-s**.

Add ous to make words. Example: extra + ane + ous = extraneous. Remember to use your spelling rules.

1. simult + ane + ous = _____
2. miscell + ane + ous = _____
3. in + sta + ant + ane + ous = _____
4. spont + ane + ous = _____

B You learned when to double the **r** in **fer**. If **fer** is stressed in a word, the **r** doubles. If **fer** is not stressed, the **r** does not double.

Write the combined words.

1. of + fer + ed = _____
2. re + fer + ing = _____
3. in + fer + ing = _____
4. dif + fer + ent = _____
5. con + fer + ed = _____
6. suf + fer + ing = _____
7. re + fer + ed = _____
8. pre + fer + ence = _____

C Some words built from **labor** and **labour** are spelled the same everywhere in the English-speaking world. The reason is that everyone uses the allomorph **labor** to make longer words. **Labor** means "work."

Read the definitions; then complete the sentences.

elaborate: When you add more detail to something, you elaborate on that thing. Something that has a lot of detail is elaborate.

laborious: A task that requires a lot of hard work is a laborious task.

laboratory: A place where scientists work is a laboratory.

collaborate: When you work on a task with somebody else, you collaborate with that person.

1. Chopping firewood is a _____ job.
2. Clare and Pat are going to _____ on a book report.
3. Martin sewed an _____ design on his shirt.
4. Dr. Garcia keeps two hundred mice in her _____ .
5. Can you _____ on your idea for saving money?

D The morphograph **ity** at the end of a word like **humanity** or **formality** is an allomorph that is usually spelled **i-t-y**. In a few words, however, it is spelled **e-t-y**.

Here's the rule: When it follows a morphograph that ends in **y** or **i**, it is spelled **e-t-y**. When it follows any other letter, it is spelled **i-t-y**. You can hear the two vowel sounds when you use **ety**.

Write each word with the allomorph ity or ety. Use your spelling rules.

1. real + ity/ety = _____
2. vary + ity/ety = _____
3. soci + ity/ety = _____
4. author + ity/ety = _____
5. propri + ity/ety = _____
6. anxi + ity/ety = _____

Lesson 108   **199**

E When you add a morphograph that begins with a vowel to some words that end in **e-r**, the final **e** drops. The following words end in **e-r**. They lose the final **e** when combined with morphographs that begin with **a, y,** or **o**.

anger	hunger	enter
disaster	register	administer
hinder	monster	wonder

Combine these morphographs that begin with a, y, and o with the words below.

1. anger + y = _____
2. monster + ous = _____
3. hinder + ance = _____
4. register + ate + ion = _____
5. wonder + ous = _____
6. disaster + ous = _____
7. hunger + y = _____
8. administer + ate + ion = _____
9. enter + ance = _____

END OF LESSON 108

Name

A

1. _____
2. _____
3. _____

B

You have already learned that related words use the allomorphs **script** and **scribe.** When the word ends in **ion** or **ive,** the allomorph **script** is used.

There are other pairs of allomorphs that work the same way as **scribe** and **script.** Here they are:

sorb and **sorpt**   **duce** and **duct**   **sume** and **sumpt**

Here are examples of how the allomorphs are used:

pro**duce**   con**sume**   ab**sorb**

pro**duct**ion   con**sumpt**ion   ab**sorpt**ion

For each word below, write a word that ends with ion.

1. introduce _____
2. assume   _____
3. absorb   _____
4. reduce   _____
5. presume   _____
6. deduce   _____

C You learned when to double the **r** in **fer**. If **fer** is stressed in a word, the **r** doubles. If **fer** is not stressed, the **r** does not double.

Write the combined words.

1. pre + fer + ed = _____
2. con + fer + ence = _____
3. dif + fer + ed = _____
4. in + fer + ing = _____
5. re + fer + ed = _____
6. of + fer + ing = _____
7. suf + fer + ed = _____
8. re + fer + al = _____

D Circle the misspelled word in each group. Then write it correctly.

1. possible
   considerable
   believible
   serviceable
   _____

2. nineteen
   ninety
   nineth
   forty-nine
   _____

3. sosiety
   personality
   variety
   identity
   _____

4. divide
   inspire
   dezire
   decision
   _____

5. expect
   exsist
   execute
   experiment
   _____

6. production
   consumption
   description
   repitition
   _____

E These words lose the final **e** when combined with a morphograph that begins with **a, y,** or **o.**

Add the morphographs to these words. Be careful. The final e only drops when the next morphograph begins with a, y, or o.

1. hunger + y = _____

2. disaster + ous = _____

3. disaster + s = _____

4. monster + ous = _____

5. hinder + ance = _____

6. enter + ance = _____

7. wonder + ous = _____

8. wonder + ful = _____

9. enter + y = _____

10. enter + ed = _____

Lesson 110 is a test lesson. There is no worksheet.

111 Name _____

A

1. _____
2. _____
3. _____

B

You learned that **nonwords** usually take the ending **ible,** not **able.**
There are exceptions. Here are the most important ones:

hospit + able = hospitable   ap + ply + ic + able = applicable
irrit + able = irritable   soci + able = sociable
capa + able = capable   ap + preci + able = appreciable

Here's a way to remember these exceptions. Nonwords like **hospit** and **applic** take other endings that begin with **a.**

For **hospit** there is **hospital.**   For **applic** there is **application** or **applicant.**
For **irrit** there is **irritate.**   For **soci** there is **social.**
For **capa** there is **capacity.**   For **appreci** there is **appreciate.**

Because **nonwords** like **hospit** and **applic** take one morphograph that begins with **a,** they take the ending **able,** not **ible.**

If you want to test a nonword, see if you can make up a real word that takes one of these endings: **al, ate, ation, ant,** or **acity.** If you can make up a word that takes one of these endings, the nonword probably takes **able,** not **ible.**

For each word below, write a word that ends in able or ible.

1. social = _____
2. terrify = _____
3. serviced = _____
4. applicant = _____
5. duration = _____
6. capacity = _____
7. respected = _____
8. irritation = _____
9. hospital = _____
10. audience = _____

Lesson 111

C For each word below, write a real word that ends in <u>ion</u>. You will use allomorphs.
Example: **exclaim = exclamation**

1. divide = _____
2. assume = _____
3. deceive = _____
4. introduce = _____
5. explain = _____
6. decide = _____
7. reveal = _____
8. absorb = _____

D You've learned allomorphs for **4, 5,** and **9.** The pairs of allomorphs are:
four, for; five, fif; nine, nin.

Use the allomorphs to write the names of the numbers below.

4th = _____
50 = _____
95 = _____
44 = _____
19 = _____
9th = _____

E In the next lesson you'll have a spelling contest. Some of the words below will be used in the contest.

| hospital | relieve | disastrous | during |
| preference | irritable | possible | entrance |

END OF LESSON 111

Lesson 111

A Sometimes it is hard to tell the spelling of vowels near the end of the word. If you say the word **author** or **stupid,** you can't hear whether the letter before the final consonant should be **a, e, i, o,** or **u.** Here's a trick. If you can add the morphograph **ity** to the end of the word, the pronunciation changes. The pronunciation often makes it easier to hear which letter comes just before the final consonant.

When we add **ity** to **author,** we get the word **authority.** We can hear the **o** before the **r.** When we add **ity** to **stupid,** we get the word **stupidity.** We can hear the **i** sound before the **d.** When we add **ity** to **legal,** we get **legality.** We can hear the **a** sound before the **l.**

In the words below, there is a letter missing near the end of each word. That letter always makes a sound "uh."

Add ity to each word, and write the whole word with the correct spelling.
Example: **stup_d = stupidity**

1. pri__r = _____
2. maj__r = _____
3. origin__l = _____
4. hum__d = _____
5. leg__l = _____

B For each word below, write a real word that ends in <u>ion</u>.

1. exclaim = _____
2. provide = _____
3. reduce = _____
4. perceive = _____
5. prescribe = _____
6. repeat = _____
7. produce = _____
8. decide = _____

C The spellings of many words tells us that the words went from Greek and Latin to French. There are different spellings of the **k** sound in Greek, Latin, and French. So we can tell the history of some words by looking at how the **k** sound is spelled.

If the **k** sound is spelled with the letters **ch,** the word originally came from Greek.

If the **k** sound is spelled with **c,** the spelling is Latin.

If the **k** sound is spelled with the letters **qu,** the spelling came from French.

The word **echo** has a **k** sound spelled with **ch,** so we use the Greek spelling for this word.

The word **captain** uses a **c** for the **k** sound. This word uses the Latin spelling of the **k** sound.

The word **technique** uses the letters **qu** for the **k** sound. This spelling comes from the French. (All the "eek" words spelled **ique** came from French.)

Some words with more than one **k** sound use different types of spelling for these sounds. The word **critique** has two **k** sounds. The first uses the Latin spelling. The second one uses the French spelling.

Words that use more than one spelling for the **k** sounds are among the most frequently misspelled words.

All the words below have two **k** sounds.

Underline the two k sounds in each word. Write the origin of the two k sounds on the lines.

Here's an example: <u>ch</u>roni<u>c</u>:   a. Greek   b. Latin

1. technique: a. _____   b. _____
2. conquer: a. _____   b. _____
3. critique: a. _____   b. _____
4. chemical: a. _____   b. _____

END OF LESSON 112

113 Name _____

A
1. _____
2. _____

B
Remember that if a nonword takes one ending that begins with **a**, it will take **able**, not **ible**.

For each word below, write a word that ends in able or ible.

1. changed = _____
2. irritate = _____
3. permissive = _____
4. appreciate = _____
5. duration = _____
6. capacity = _____
7. considerate = _____
8. applicant = _____

C
Write the correct spelling for each word in the **word** column.
Then write **O** or **B** after each number in the **rule** column.

Write **O** if the word is spelled by just putting the morphographs together.
Write **B** if the **fer** doubling rule explains why the spelling is changed.

rule		word
1. _____	pre + fer + s =	_____
2. _____	pre + fer + ence =	_____
3. _____	in + fer + ed =	_____
4. _____	dif + fer + ent =	_____
5. _____	re + fer + ing =	_____
6. _____	suf + fer + ed =	_____
7. _____	con + fer + ed =	_____
8. _____	of + fer + ing =	_____

Lesson 113

D The morphograph **loge** is very important. **Loge** comes from Greek, and it means "the word or name of something."

You have learned that **logic** is a single-morphograph word. Actually it is two morphographs—**loge** plus **ic.** When we combine these morphographs, the final **e** on **loge** drops, and we have the word **logic.**

Below are some other words that contain **loge:**

apologize = apo + loge + ize   analogy = ana + loge + y

Some words refer to the name of different studies. These words contain the morphograph **loge:**

Biology is the study of living things.

Astrology is the study of stars.

Geology is the study of the earth.

In all these words, the morphograph **loge** is followed by **y.** So the final **e** drops and the ending is spelled **logy.** These words tell the name for different studies.

Answer these items.

1. If **psycho** means "mind," what does the word **psychology** name? _____

2. If **entomo** means "insects," write the word that means "the study of insects." _____

3. If **anthropo** means "mankind," write the word that means "the study of mankind." _____

4. If **socio** means "a group of people," write the word that means "the study of people." _____

5. If **chrono** means "time," write the word that means "the study of time." _____

E You learned a procedure for figuring out the vowel near the end of words. If you add the morphograph **ity** to the word, the pronunciation changes, and you may be able to hear the vowel sound.

In the words below, there is a letter missing near the end of each word. That letter always makes a sound "uh."

Add ity to each word, and write the whole word with the correct spelling.

Example: leg__l = legality

1. actu__l   = _____
2. hospit__l = _____
3. stup__d   = _____
4. hum__n   = _____
5. pri__r   = _____

END OF LESSON 113

Name _____ 114

A

1. _____   4. _____
2. _____   5. _____
3. _____   6. _____

B

Remember that if a nonword takes one ending that begins with **a**, it will take **able**, not **ible**.

For each word below, write a word that ends in <u>able</u> or <u>ible</u>.

1. hospitality = _____   5. social   = _____
2. credit   = _____   6. denial   = _____
3. capacity   = _____   7. audience   = _____
4. vision   = _____   8. replacement = _____

C

In Lesson 113 you learned that **loge** means "word or name." Many names of different studies contain **loge**, like the word **geology**.

Answer these items.

1. **Ornitho** means "bird." Write the word that means "the study of birds."   _____

2. **Morpho** means "form." Write the word that means "the study of forms."   _____

3. **Techno** means "skill." Write the word that means "the study of skills."   _____

4. **Theo** means "gods." Write the word that means "the study of gods, or religion."   _____

Lesson 114   211

D The allomorphs **here** and **hese** mean "to stick." Here are some words that use **here** and **hese**.

adhere: To stick to something is to adhere to it.

adhesive: Something that sticks to things is adhesive.

cohesive: Things that stick together are cohesive.

coherent: When something makes sense, it is coherent.

hesitate: When something pauses, or sticks in time, it hesitates.

hesitant: Something that hesitates is hesitant.

Write the morphographs for each word.

1. _____ + _____ + _____ = adhered

2. _____ + ite + _____ = hesitate

3. _____ + _____ + _____ + _____ = incoherent

4. _____ + _____ + _____ = hesitant

5. _____ + _____ + _____ = adherent

6. _____ + _____ + _____ = cohesive

An e or an a is missing from each word below. Write each word using the correct vowel.

7. hesit__nt = _____

8. coher__nce = _____

9. hesit__ncy = _____

10. adher__nt = _____

Lesson 114

Find the ten misspelled words in the student's answer. Then write them correctly.

Mr. Mortenson was retired from his job as a construction contractor. He had made a lot of money, but he knew that many other people suffered because of extreme poverty. He decided to join with a group of people who built houses for people who could not afford to build a house of their own. The family that would live in the new house helped build it, so they really appreciated it. The people in the building group, however, helped themselves, not just the new home owners. They learned that they were happiest when they weren't greedy and selfish. They believed that selflessness was a benefit to everyone.

Describe Mr. Mortenson.

    Mr. Mortenson was a retired construcsion contracter. Although he had money, he knew that many peeple suffered from poverty. He desided to help by building houses for poor people. He beleived that selflessnes benufited both the people who got the houses and the people who built them. He was happyest when he was unselfushly helping other people. The people who got the new homes appreshiated them.

_____

_____

_____

_____

_____

_____

_____

_____

_____

_____

Lesson 115 is a test lesson. There is no worksheet.

116 Name _____

A

1. _____   5. _____
2. _____   6. _____
3. _____   7. _____
4. _____   8. _____

B

In the words below, there is a letter missing near the end of each word. That letter always makes a sound "uh."

Add ity to each word, and write the whole word with the correct spelling.

Example: **person__l = personality**

1. re__l   = _____
2. maj__r   = _____
3. leg__l   = _____
4. hum__d   = _____
5. auth__r = _____

C

Write the morphographs for each word. Remember to put a + between them.

1. occur   _____
2. geologist   _____
3. biography   _____
4. biology   _____
5. apology   _____
6. changeable   _____
7. scientist   _____
8. conceivable _____

Lesson 116

D Words like **due** and **true** do not follow the final-**e** rule. When we add a morphograph that begins with a consonant to the end of these words, we drop the final **e**. **Due + ly** is spelled **duly**. **True + th** is spelled **truth**.

The strange spellings of these words came about because of something that happened about six hundred years ago. At that time, there were no printing presses. All books were written by people. The people who made copies of books were called scribes. For some reason scribes did not like words that end in **u** or **w**. Some words that they copied did end in **u** or **w**. At that time **due** was spelled **du**, and **true** was spelled **tru**. The scribes added the final **e** to these words. But the scribes did not add the final **e** to words like **truth** and **duty**.

So remember that words like **truth** and **duty** do not follow the final-**e** rule. These words are spelled as they used to be spelled. But **due** and **true** are newer spellings.

Add the morphographs together.

1. due + ly   = _____
2. true + th = _____
3. due + ty   = _____
4. true + ly = _____

The word **argue** used to be spelled **argu**. The word **awe** used to be spelled **aw**. The words below do not follow the final-**e** rule.

Add the morphographs together.

5. argue + ment = _____
6. awe + ful   = _____

E Make 7 real words from the morphographs in the box. Use the <u>fer</u> doubling rule.

| re | dif | fer | pre | ence | ed |

1. _____   5. _____
2. _____   6. _____
3. _____   7. _____
4. _____

END OF LESSON 116

117 Name

A

1. _____
2. _____
3. _____

B

You have learned that adding **ity** can change the pronunciation of a word. Sometimes adding **ity** also changes the spelling. Here's how the spelling changes with **ous, able,** and **ible:**

ous + ity = osity   The **u** drops. You can hear the **o** sound in **osity.**
able + ity = ability   An **i** is added. You can hear it.
ible + ity = ibility   An **i** is added. You can hear it.

Add the morphograph ity to these words.

1. curious = _____
2. probable = _____
3. visible = _____
4. generous = _____
5. disable = _____
6. possible = _____

C

You learned about words like **truly** and **argument.** When we add a morphograph that begins with a consonant, we drop the final **e.**

Write the morphographs for each word.

1. _____ + th + _____ = truthful
2. _____ + ly = duly
3. _____ + ment = argument
4. _____ + ty = duty
5. _____ + ful + _____ = awfully
6. _____ + ly = truly

Lesson 117

D The word-history passage in Lesson 116 told about the scribes and how they changed the spellings of words that end in **u** or **w**. The scribes added a final **e** to these words. At the time there were other words, like **giv** and **hav**. These words were spelled the way they were pronounced. The scribes put an **e** on the end of them. But the pronunciation did not change. Today some words that end in **v-e** are spelled the way they sound: **save, stove.** Other words that end in **v-e** are not spelled the way they sound: **have, give.** Although these words follow the final-**e** rule, their pronunciation is strange.

Read the words below. In column 1, write the words that are spelled the way they sound. If you say the letter name of the vowel in the middle of the word, write the word in column 1. In column 2, write the words that are not spelled the way they sound.

love	behave	glove
crave	have	hive
stove	give	

1

_____

_____

_____

_____

2

_____

_____

_____

_____

E In the next lesson, you'll have a spelling contest.
Some of the words below will be used in the contest.

irritate	behave	believe	biology
major	noticeable	technique	truly
ability	hesitate	argument	ninth

END OF LESSON 117

A

Here's how the spelling changes when we add **ity** to **ous**, **able**, and **ible**:

ous + ity = osity   The **u** drops. You can hear the **o** sound in **osity**.
able + ity = ability   An **i** is added. You can hear it.
ible + ity = ibility   An **i** is added. You can hear it.

Add the morphograph ity to these words.

1. responsible = _____
2. desirable = _____
3. monstrous = _____
4. durable = _____
5. stable = _____
6. compatible = _____

B

Write the correct word for each sentence.

1. The **plain/plane** changed its **coarse/course**.   _____

2. That equipment is not portable; it's **stationary/stationery**.   _____

3. The suitcase blocked the **aisle/isle**.   _____

4. The smog **affects/effects** my **sight/site**.   _____

5. The garbage trucks take **waist/waste** to a disposal **sight/site**.   _____

C You learned that some words that end in **v-e** are spelled the way they sound: **save, stove.** Other words that end in **v-e** are not spelled the way they sound: **have, give.** Although these words follow the final-**e** rule, their pronunciation is strange.

Read the words below. In column 1, write the words that are spelled the way they sound. If you say the letter name of the vowel in the middle of the word, write the word in column 1. In column 2, write the words that are not spelled the way they sound.

```
five        give        grave
save        have        move
love        cove
```

1

_____   _____

_____   _____

_____   _____

_____   _____

END OF LESSON 118

A

1. _____
2. _____
3. _____

B The morphograph **ize** means "to make" or "to make more of something." **Ize** is used in words like **formalize, civilize, organize,** and **legalize.**

Ize is a very old morphograph that can be traced back to Latin and Greek words. The French also used this morphograph, but they changed the spelling to **ise.** Because some of our words come from Latin and others come from French, we have both **i-z-e** and **i-s-e** spellings in English.

Although both spellings are used in English, there is a rule for deciding whether the word is spelled with **ize** or **ise.** Here's the rule: Use **ize.**

This rule works for just about every word. Some words may be spelled with either **ise** or **ize.** For example, both **organize** and **organise** are acceptable spellings. For words that can be spelled both ways, the **ize** spelling is preferred.

Some words cannot be spelled both ways. Nearly all these end in **ize: computerize, modernize, legalize,** and many others. So if you use **ize,** you'll spell these words correctly.

By using **ize,** you'll spell thousands of words correctly. There are only two exceptions: **chastise,** which means "to scold," and **advertise.**

Combine the morphographs. Use ise only if you can't use ize.

1. ad + vert + ize/ise = _____
2. organ + ize/ise + ate + ion = _____
3. critic + ize/ise = _____
4. real + ize/ise = _____
5. hospital + ize/ise = _____
6. author + ize/ise + ate + ion = _____

You have learned that **nonwords** usually take the ending **ible** and that **words** usually take the ending **able**. You also learned that there are some **nonwords** that take **able**. **Able** is added to **nonwords** if there is a form of the word that ends in **al, ate,** or some other morphograph that begins with **a**.

Another group of exceptions is made of **words** that take **ible**. The words in this group are among the most frequently misspelled words. Even good spellers tend to add **able**—not **ible**—to words.

Here are some of the more important **words** that take **ible**:

force	+ ible = forcible	compress	+ ible = compressible
convert	+ ible = convertible	exhaust	+ ible = exhaustible
reduce	+ ible = reducible	deduct	+ ible = deductible
reverse	+ ible = reversible	resist	+ ible = resistible
response	+ ible = responsible	sense	+ ible = sensible
corrupt	+ ible = corruptible		

For any words that take **ible,** there is a form of the word that ends in **ion** or **ive**. These morphographs begin with **i**.

For **exhaust** there is **exhaustive** or **exhaustion**. For **compress** there is **compression**.
For **deduct** there is **deductive** or **deduction**. For **resist** there is **resistive**.
For **reverse** there is **reversion**. For **response** there is **responsive**.
For **corrupt** there is **corruption**.

Finding words that end in the morphograph **ion** or **ive** helps with some of the **ible** words. But it does not help with all of them. There is no rule for helping you spell **sensible,** and it is one of the most important words that end in **ible**. Study the **ible** words in the list above. Make sure that you know how to spell **sensible** and **responsible**. You will use these words frequently.

Write each word with the morphograph <u>able</u> or <u>ible</u>. Some morphographs have already been combined. Use your spelling rules.

1. response + able/ible = _____
2. service + able/ible = _____
3. applic + able/ible = _____
4. invince + able/ible = _____
5. sense + able/ible = _____
6. ter + able/ible = _____
7. irresponse + able/ible = _____
8. knowledge + able/ible = _____

D The morphograph **vive** means "to live." Here are some words that use the morphograph **vive**.

survive: When you live through something, you survive it.

revive: When you bring something back to life, you revive it.

vivacious: Someone who is very lively is vivacious.

vivid: Something that is very bright and easy to see is vivid.

Write the morphographs for each word.

1. _____ + _____ + _____ = survivor
2. _____ + ace + _____ = vivacious
3. _____ + _____ + _____ = revival
4. _____ + id = vivid
5. _____ + _____ + _____ = survivable

Write the correct words using vive.

6. When he fainted, the nurse _____ him with smelling salts.

7. After the ship sank, one _____ drifted to an island.

8. The light was so _____ she had to close her eyes.

9. People always had a lot of fun when she was around because she was so _____ .

Lesson 120 is a test lesson. This is the last worksheet in Grade 5.

Word Parts

a — act

a	achieve
	across
	amusement
	amusing
	arise
	around
ab	abrupt
	abruptly
	absent
	absorbed
	absorption
able	ability
	admirable
	applicable
	appreciable
	believable
	capability
	capable
	changeable
	chargeable
	conceivable
	considerable
	considerably
	deniable
	desirability
	desirable
	disability
	durability
	durable
	enjoyable
	establish
	establishment
	exchangeable
	excitable
	hospitable
	inconceivable
	incurable
	indescribable
	indispensable
	innumerable
	irritable
	justifiable
	knowledgeable
	manageable
	noticeable
	objectionable
	pliable
	portable
	predictable
	predictably
	preferable
	probability
	probably
	questionable
	reestablish
	regrettable
	reliable
	replaceable
	respectable
	reusable
	serviceable
	sociable
	stability
	stable
	survivable
	traceable
	unbreakable
	uncontrollable
	undeniable
	undeniably
	undesirable
	unforgettable
	unjustifiable
	unquestionable
	usable
	valuable
	variability
	variable
ac	accommodate
	accommodation
	accommodations
	accompaniment
	accompany
	account
	accounted
	accounting
	acknowledge
	acknowledged
	acquaintance
	acquainted
	acquire
	acquired
	acquiring
	acquit
	acquittal
	acquitted
	acquitting
ace	ace
	vivacious
ache	backache
act	action
	actions
	activity
	actor
	actuality
	actually
	radioactive
	reaction

Word Parts

ad

ad
- adequate
- adhere
- adhered
- adherent
- adhesive
- administration
- admirable
- admire
- admission
- admit
- admittance
- admitted
- admitting
- advantage
- advantageous
- advertise
- advice
- advise
- advised
- disadvantage

af
- affect
- affected
- affection
- affectionate
- affects
- affluent
- unaffected

age
- advantage
- advantageous
- baggage
- carriage
- courage
- courageous
- disadvantage
- encourage
- encouraging
- espionage
- leakage
- leverage
- manage
- manageable
- managed
- management
- manager
- managerial
- marriage
- mismanage
- mismanaged
- package
- passage
- patronage
- storage
- usage

agony
- agonize
- agony
- antagonize

ain
- captain
- certain

air
- airport

aire
- questionnaire

al
- acquittal
- allocate
- allotment
- allotted
- allowed
- animal
- animals
- antisocial
- astronomical
- athletically
- autobiographical
- burial
- central
- chemical
- chemicals
- commensalism
- critical

al
- critically
- decentralize
- deferral
- denial
- departmental
- equal
- equalize
- equally
- experimental
- fatal
- final
- finally
- formal
- graphically
- historical
- hospital
- hospitality
- hospitalize
- hospitalized
- hymnal
- hysterical
- ideal
- impersonal
- industrial
- informal
- legality
- local
- localize
- magical
- manual
- manually
- mechanical
- mistrial
- mystical
- noncommittal
- numeral
- numerical
- occasional
- occasionally
- original

al

	originality
	pedal
	personal
	personality
	personalize
	personalized
	philosophical
	physical
	physically
	principal
	professional
	punctual
	quizzical
	radial
	referral
	refusal
	reversal
	revival
	rhetorical
	rhythmical
	sentimental
	signal
	social
	socialize
	spiral
	trial
	trivial
	universal
	unoriginal
example	example
an	anonymous
	another
	historian
	humanity
ance	acquaintance
	admittance
	appearance
	appliance
	clearance
	compliance
	disappearance
	distance
	distances
	endurance
	entrance
	grievance
	hesitancy
	hindrance
	importance
	performance
	performances
	relevance
	remittance
	vacancy
	variance
anchor	anchored
ane	extraneous
	instantaneous
	miscellaneous
	simultaneous
	spontaneous
anger	anger
	angry
anima	animal
	animals
	unanimous
	unanimously
answer	answer
ant	antiperspirant
	applicant
	constant
	constantly
	equidistant
	hesitant
	immigrant
	immigrants
	important

ap

	instant
	instantaneous
	irrelevant
	malignant
	migrant
	migrants
	militant
	pleasant
	radiant
	relevant
	resistant
	significant
	substantial
	unpleasant
	vacant
ante	antecedent
	antique
anti	antagonize
	antibodies
	antibody
	antiperspirant
	antisocial
	antonym
anxi	anxiety
	anxious
ap	appear
	appearance
	appeared
	appearing
	appliance
	applicable
	applicant
	application
	applied
	apply
	applying
	appreciable
	appreciate

Word Parts

Word Parts

ap

	appreciation
	apprehensive
	approach
	approached
	disappear
	disappearance
	disappeared
	disappearing
	disappoint
	disappointed
	unappreciative
apo	apologize
	apologized
	apology
	apostrophe
ar	arrangement
	familiar
	familiarize
	summarization
	summarize
	summary
arch	patriarch
argue	argue
	argument
art	art
ary	contrary
	dictionaries
	dictionary
	disciplinary
	imaginary
	military
	stationary
as	associate
	association
	assumed
	assumption
	fantasies

	fantastic
	fantasy
	whereas
aster	asterisk
	disaster
	disasters
	disastrous
astro	astrologer
	astrology
	astronaut
	astronomer
	astronomers
	astronomical
	astronomy
ate	accommodate
	accommodation
	accommodations
	adequate
	administration
	affectionate
	allocate
	application
	appreciate
	appreciation
	associate
	association
	authorization
	calculations
	certificate
	certification
	characterization
	citation
	civilization
	classification
	collaborate
	compensate
	complicate
	concentrate
	concentration

ate

concentrations
conservation
consideration
conversation
depreciate
depreciates
depreciation
deviate
deviation
dictate
dictation
dictator
dislocate
dissociate
duration
educate
educator
elaborate
elevation
elevator
emigrate
emigrated
enumerate
equate
equation
equator
evacuate
evacuated
exclamation
expectation
explanation
fortunate
hesitate
hyphenated
identification
imagination
imaginations
imaginative
immigrate
impersonate

Word Parts

ate

- inconsiderate
- information
- informative
- infuriate
- inspiration
- irritate
- irritated
- justification
- laboratory
- locate
- location
- manifestation
- manipulate
- migrate
- migration
- migratory
- moderate
- moderator
- multiplication
- observation
- organization
- originate
- originator
- presentation
- proclamation
- pulsate
- punctuate
- punctuation
- quotation
- radiate
- radiation
- radiator
- registration
- relocate
- reservation
- respiration
- revelation
- rheumatism
- schematic
- separate
- separation
- sophisticated
- state
- statement
- station
- stationery
- summarization
- summation
- unappreciative
- unfortunate
- unfortunately
- unification
- vacate
- vacation
- verification
- versatile
- versatility

athlete
- athlete
- athletic
- athletically
- athletics

audi
- audience
- audible
- audition
- auditor

author
- authority
- authorization
- authorize

auto
- autobiographer
- autobiographical
- autobiography
- autograph
- autographs
- automotive

awe
- awe
- awful
- awfully

baby
- babies

bene

back
- backache

bag
- baggage
- bagged
- bagging

bake
- baker
- bakers
- bakes
- baking

bank
- bankrupt

bare
- barely

base
- basement
- basic

be
- begin
- beginner
- beginning
- behave
- behind
- belief
- believable
- believe
- believed
- believer
- believes
- believing
- disbelief

beam
- beam

beauty
- beautiful
- beautify

beggar
- beggar

bel
- bellicose
- belligerent
- rebel
- rebellion
- rebels

bene
- benediction
- benefactor

Word Parts

bene

	beneficial	**busy**	busily		precedent
	benefit		business		preceding
	benefits		businesses		procedure
	benevolent		busy		recede
	benign	**calcule**	calculations		receding
bi	bicycle	**capa**	capability	**ceed**	exceed
	bicyclist		capable		exceeded
biblio	bibliography	**car**	car		exceeding
bid	bidden	**care**	careless		exceedingly
	forbid	**carry**	carriage		proceed
	forbidden		carrier		proceeded
big	biggest		carries		proceeding
bio	autobiographical		carrying		proceedings
	autobiography	**case**	casual		proceeds
	biography		casually		succeed
	biology		casualty		succeeded
blame	blameless		occasion		succeeding
body	antibodies		occasional	**ceive**	conceivable
	antibody		occasionally		deceive
box	boxer		occasions		deceived
boy	boyish	**category**	categories		deceiving
break	unbreakable		categorize		inconceivable
breath	breath		category		misconceive
	breathless	**caught**	caught		perceive
	breathlessness	**caut**	caution		perceived
breathe	breathe		cautious		receive
bridge	bridge		precaution		received
brother	brother	**cede**	antecedent		receiver
build	build		concede		receiving
	building		conceded	**cel**	excel
bury	burial		concedes		excelled
	buried		conceding		excellence
	bury		interceded		excellent
	burying		precede	**centre**	central
			preceded		concentrate
			precedence		concentration
					decentralize
					eccentric

centre

228 Word Parts

Word Parts

cept

cept	conception
	deception
	deceptive
	except
	misconception
	perception
	perceptive
	preconception
	reception
	receptive
	susceptible
ceros	rhinoceros
cert	certain
	certificate
	certification
	certified
	certify
	certifying
	concert
	disconcert
cess	excessive
	excessively
	process
	success
	successful
	unsuccessful
challenge	challenge
	challenged
change	changeable
	changing
	exchangeable
character	character
	characteristic
	characterization
	characterize
charge	chargeable
chaste	chastise

cheme	chemical
	chemicals
	chemistry
chief	mischief
chieve	achieve
	mischievous
choly	melancholy
chord	chords
chore	chorus
cide	decide
	decided
cipe	principal
ciple	disciple
	disciplinary
	discipline
	principles
circle	semicircle
cise	decision
	decisive
	exercise
	exercises
	exercising
cite	citation
	excitable
	excite
	excited
civil	civil
	civilian
	civilization
	civilize
claim	exclaim
clame	exclamation
	proclamation

com

class	classification
	classified
	classify
	classifying
clear	clearance
close	close
	closed
	enclosure
cloth	cloth
clothe	clothe
	clothes
cloud	cloudy
clude	conclude
	exclude
	include
cluse	conclusion
	conclusions
	conclusive
	exclusion
	exclusive
	inclusive
co	coherence
	coherent
	cohesive
	incoherent
coarse	coarse
	coarsely
col	collaborate
	collection
colon	colony
	semicolon
com	accommodate
	accommodation
	accommodations
	accompaniment

Word Parts

com

- accompany
- commensalism
- commit
- commitment
- committed
- committee
- commodity
- commotion
- companies
- companion
- company
- compare
- compatibility
- compatible
- compelled
- compelling
- compensate
- compete
- competent
- competition
- competitor
- competitors
- completely
- compliance
- complicate
- complied
- comply
- complying
- comprehension
- compress
- compressible
- compression
- compromise
- computer
- noncommittal
- recommend
- recommended

come

- coming
- welcome

comma

- comma

con

- concede
- conceded
- concedes
- conceding
- conceivable
- concentrate
- concentration
- concentrations
- conception
- concert
- conclude
- conclusion
- conclusions
- conclusive
- concur
- concurred
- concurrence
- concurrent
- concurs
- conductor
- confer
- conference
- conferred
- confined
- confusing
- confusion
- conquer
- conquest
- conscience
- conscientious
- conscious
- consecutive
- consents
- conservation
- consider
- considerable
- considerably
- consideration
- consist
- consisted
- consistency
- consistent
- conspicuous
- conspire
- constant
- constantly
- consumption
- contain
- contained
- container
- continue
- continued
- continuous
- control
- controlled
- controlling
- conversation
- converse
- convertible
- convince
- discontent
- discontinue
- inconceivable
- inconsiderate
- inconsistent
- misconceive
- misconception
- preconception
- unconscious
- uncontrollable

contra

- contradict
- contradicted
- contradiction
- contradicts
- contrary

copy

- copied
- copying

cor

cor	correctly
	corrupt
	corruptible
	corruption
cosmo	cosmonaut
count	account
	accounted
	accounting
could	could
cour	courage
	courageous
	encourage
	encouraging
cove	cove
cover	covered
	discovered
	discoveries
	recovered
	uncover
	undiscovered
crave	crave
crease	increases
create	create
	created
	creation
	creator
	creature
crede	credible
	credit
	incredible
critic	critic
	critical
	critically
	criticism
	criticize

critique	critique
cross	across
cry	cried
	crier
	cry
	crying
cur	concur
	concurred
	concurrence
	concurrent
	concurs
	currency
	current
	currently
	curtail
	occur
	occurred
	occurrence
	occurrences
	occurs
	recur
	recurred
	recurrence
	recurrences
	recurrent
	recurring
	recurs
cure	curiosity
	curious
	incurable
	manicure
	pedicure
cycle	bicycle
	bicyclist
	cyclic
	cyclone
	tricycle
	unicycle

de

danger	dangerous
day	day
de	deceive
	deceived
	deceiving
	decentralize
	deception
	deceptive
	decide
	decided
	decision
	decisive
	deduct
	deductible
	deduction
	deductive
	defer
	deferral
	define
	defined
	definite
	definitely
	definition
	deject
	deluxe
	demote
	department
	departmental
	deport
	deported
	depreciate
	depreciates
	depreciation
	describe
	describes
	descript
	description
	descriptive
	desirability

Word Parts

de   **dure**

	desirable		contradicts		discoveries
	desire		dictate		disease
	desirous		dictation		diseased
	despise		dictator		dislocate
	destroyed		diction		dispel
	deter		dictionaries		disruptive
	deviate		dictionary		dissent
	deviation		edict		dissociate
	devise		indict		indispensable
	indefinite		indicted		undiscovered
	indefinitely		indictment	**drive**	driver
	indescribable		malediction		drivers
	undefined		predict		drives
	undesirable		predictable		driving
dense	density		predictably	**dry**	drying
deny	deniable		predicting	**duce**	educate
	denial		prediction		educator
	denied	**dif**	differ		introduce
	deny		differed		introduced
	denying		difference		produced
	undeniable		different		reduced
	undeniably	**dis**	disability		reducible
di	direct		disadvantage	**duct**	conductor
	direction		disappear		deduct
	directly		disappearance		deductible
	distance		disappeared		deduction
	distances		disappearing		deductive
	divide		disappoint		introduction
	divided		disappointed		production
	divider		disaster		reduction
	divisible		disasters		viaduct
	division		disastrous	**due**	due
	equidistant		disbelief		duly
	individual		disciple		duty
dict	benediction		disciplinary	**Dutch**	Dutch
	contradict		discipline	**dure**	durability
	contradicted		discontent		durable
	contradiction		discontinue		
			discovered		

dure

	duration
	during
	endurance
	endure
	endured
	enduring
e	edict
	educate
	educator
	elaborate
	elevation
	elevator
	emigrate
	emigrated
	enumerate
	equip
	equipment
	equipped
	erosion
	eruption
	espionage
	establish
	establishment
	evacuate
	evacuated
	event
	eventual
	reestablish
each	each
early	earlier
	earliest
earn	earn
ease	disease
	diseased
	easier
	easiest
	easy
eat	eating

ec	eccentric
echo	echo
	echoes
eco	economic
ee	committee
ef	effect
	effective
	effectively
	effort
	effortless
el	model
	personnel
embarrass	embarrass
	embarrassed
	embarrasses
	embarrassment
en	bidden
	enclosure
	encourage
	encouraging
	endurance
	endure
	endured
	enduring
	enjoy
	enjoyable
	enjoyed
	enjoyment
	enlightening
	flatten
	forbidden
	forgiven
	forgotten
	forsaken
	given
	gotten
	happen

ent

	happens
	hidden
	mistaken
	taken
	unenlightened
ence	audience
	coherence
	concurrence
	conference
	conscience
	consistency
	currency
	difference
	equivalence
	excellence
	existence
	experience
	inexperienced
	inference
	influence
	influenced
	occurrence
	occurrences
	precedence
	preference
	recurrence
	recurrences
	reference
	science
	sentence
	sentenced
end	horrendous
	stupendous
	tremendous
ent	adherent
	affluent
	antecedent
	belligerent
	benevolent

Word Parts

ent

coherent
competent
concurrent
conscientious
consistent
current
currently
different
equivalent
excellent
expedient
fluent
fluently
incoherent
inconsistent
influential
insistent
malevolent
nonexistent
nutrient
persistent
precedent
recurrent
repellent
residents
scientific
scientist

enter

entered
enterprise
entertain
entertainer
entertainment
entrance
entry

equi

adequate
equal
equalize
equally
equate
equation
equator
equidistant
equinox
equivalence
equivalent

er

astrologer
astronomer
astronomers
baker
bakers
beginner
believer
belligerent
boxer
carrier
computer
container
crier
divider
driver
drivers
earlier
easier
entertainer
exercise
exercises
exercising
geographer
happier
healthier
hindrance
lever
luckier
manager
managerial
manufacturer
misnomer
moderate

er

moderator
mysterious
mysteriously
mystery
noisier
performer
photographer
player
porter
prayer
propeller
quitter
receiver
reporter
reviewer
revolver
robber
robberies
runner
sadder
server
shipper
shopper
shoppers
sorer
stationery
stranger
sunnier
swimmer
swimmers
thievery
voter
waiter
washer
waxier
weaker
wittier
wolverine
worker
workers

er   **fame**

	wrapper	**ever**	every			expansion
	wrappers		whatever			expect
	writer		whatsoever			expectation
ern	modern		whoever			expecting
	modernize		whomever			expedient
est	biggest	**ex**	example			expedite
	driest		exceed			expedition
	earliest		exceeded			expeditious
	easiest		exceeding			expend
	fanciest		exceedingly			expense
	friendliest		excel			expenses
	greatest		excelled			expensive
	happiest		excellence			experience
	heaviest		excellent			experiment
	hottest		except			experimental
	interest		excessive			expire
	interesting		excessively			explain
	luckiest		exchangeable			explanation
	modest		excitable			export
	modestly		excite			exports
	modesty		excited			expressive
	nastiest		exclaim			extension
	saddest		exclamation			extraction
	sorest		exclude			extractor
	strangest		exclusion			inexperienced
	sturdiest		exclusive			nonexistent
	sunniest		execute	**exam**	exam
	waxiest		execution	**extra**	extraneous
	whitest		executive	**face**	surface
	widest		exercise		surfaced
	wittiest		exercises	**fact**	benefactor
eth	fortieth		exercising		factories
	ninetieth		exhaust		manufacture
ety	anxiety		exhaustible		manufacturer
	propriety		exhaustion	**fail**	failure
	societies		exhaustive	**false**	falsify
	society		exist	**fame**	famous
	variety		existence		
			exit		
			expand		

Word Parts

family | | | for

family	familiar		infer	**fine**	confined
	familiarize		inference		define
	family		inferred		defined
fancy	fanciest		inferring		definite
	fancy		offer		definitely
fant	fantasies		offered		definition
	fantastic		offering		final
	fantasy		prefer		finally
farm	farming		preferable		fined
fat	fatty		preference		finish
fate	fatal		preferred		finite
fect	affect		preferring		indefinite
	affected		prefers		indefinitely
	affection		refer		infinite
	affectionate		reference		infinitely
	affects		referral		refining
	effect		referred		undefined
	effective		referring	**fit**	benefit
	effectively		suffer		benefits
	infection		suffered	**five**	five
	perfect		suffering		ninety-five
	unaffected		transfer	**fix**	prefix
fend	defend		transferred		unfixed
	offend	**fess**	profess	**flat**	flatten
fense	defensive		profession	**flu**	affluent
	offensive		professional		flu
fer	confer	**fest**	manifestation		fluent
	conference	**fice**	beneficial		fluently
	conferred		office		fluid
	defer		official		influence
	deferral		sacrifice		influenced
	differ		sacrificial		influential
	differed	**fif**	fifteen		influenza
	difference		fifth		superfluous
	different		fifties	**for**	forbid
	ferry		fifty		forbidden
		find	find		forgetting
			findings		

236   Word Parts

for

	forgive
	forgiven
	forgiveness
	forgot
	forgotten
	forsake
	forsaken
	forties
	fortieth
	forty
	forty-four
	forty-ninth
	unforgettable
force	forcible
form	formal
	formless
	inform
	informal
	information
	informative
	informing
	misinformed
	performance
	performances
	performed
	performer
	performing
	reformed
	transform
	transformed
	uniform
	uninformed
fort	effort
	effortless
	fort
	fortify
	fortunate
	fortune
	misfortune
	unfortunate
	unfortunately
four	forty-four
	four
	fours
	fourteen
	fourteenth
	fourth
	ninety-fourth
friend	friend
	friendliest
	friendliness
	friendly
	friends
ful	awful
	awfully
	beautiful
	helpful
	hopeful
	hopefully
	joyful
	pitiful
	playful
	regretful
	resourceful
	successful
	thoughtful
	truthful
	unsuccessful
	useful
	wasteful
	wonderful
fun	funny
fury	furious
	fury
	infuriate
fuse	confusing
	confusion

graph

	refusal
	refuse
	refused
gave	gave
gener	generosity
	generous
geo	geographer
	geographic
	geography
	geologist
	geology
get	forget
	forgetting
	unforgettable
gin	begin
	beginner
	beginning
give	forgive
	forgiven
	forgiveness
	give
	given
glory	glorified
	glorify
	glorious
glove	glove
got	forgot
	forgotten
	gotten
grace	grace
	gracious
	graciousness
graph	autobiographer
	autobiographical
	autobiography
	autograph

Word Parts 237

Word Parts

graph / **hunger**

	autographs		happier		hesitant
	bibliography		happiest		hesitate
	biography		happily	hi	historian
	geographer		happiness		historic
	geographic		happy		historical
	geography		mishap		history
	graph		mishaps		prehistoric
	graphic		perhaps	hid	hidden
	graphically		unhappy	hind	behind
	graphics	hard	hard		hindrance
	graphite	hat	hats	hive	hive
	graphs	haust	exhaust	hood	likelihood
	morphograph		exhaustible	hop	hop
	morphographs		exhaustion		hopped
	paragraph		exhaustive	hope	hope
	phonograph	have	behave		hopeful
	photograph		have		hopefully
	photographer	hazard	haphazard		hopeless
	photographic		hazardous		hopelessly
	photographs		hazards		hoping
	photography	heal	health	hor	horrendous
	telegraph		healthier		horrible
grave	grave		healthy		horrid
great	great		unhealthy		horrify
	greatest	heavy	heaviest	hospit	hospitable
	greatly		heaviness		hospital
gret	regret	help	helpful		hospitality
	regretful	here	adhere		hospitalize
	regrettable		adhered		hospitalized
grief	grief		adherent	hot	hottest
grieve	grievance		coherence	house	warehouses
	grieved		coherent	hume	humanity
grow	growth		incoherent		humidity
gym	gym	hese	adhesive	hunger	hunger
hap	haphazard		cohesive		hungry
	happen		hesitancy		
	happens				

238 Word Parts

hurry

hurry	hurried
	hurrying
hymn	hymn
	hymnal
hyphen	hyphen
	hyphenated
hyster	hysterical
ial	beneficial
	impartial
	influential
	judicial
	managerial
	official
	partial
	partially
	prejudicial
	sacrificial
ian	civilian
	magician
	musician
	pedestrian
	physician
ible	audible
	compatibility
	compatible
	compressible
	convertible
	corruptible
	credible
	deductible
	divisible
	exhaustible
	forcible
	horrible
	incredible
	invincible
	invisible
	irresponsible
	legible
	permissible
	possibility
	possible
	reducible
	resistible
	responsibility
	responsible
	reversible
	sensible
	susceptible
	transmissible
	terrible
	visibility
	visible
ic	applicable
	applicant
	application
	astronomical
	athletic
	athletically
	athletics
	autobiographical
	basic
	bellicose
	certificate
	certification
	characteristic
	chemical
	chemicals
	classification
	complicate
	cyclic
	eccentric
	economic
	geographic
	graphic
	graphically

ice

	graphics
	historic
	historical
	hysterical
	identification
	justification
	logic
	mechanic
	mechanical
	mechanics
	multiplication
	music
	musician
	mystical
	numerical
	patriotic
	philosophical
	photographic
	prehistoric
	quizzical
	replica
	rhetoric
	rhetorical
	rhythmic
	rhythmical
	schematic
	scientific
	significant
	sophisticated
	symbolic
	terrific
	unification
	verification
ice	justice
	malice
	malicious
	notice
	noticeable
	service

Word Parts

ice

- serviceable
- simplicity
- unnoticed

id
- fluid
- horrid
- humidity
- stupid
- stupidity
- valid
- vivid

idea
- ideal

ident
- identical
- identification
- identified
- identify
- identifying
- identity

ify
- beautify
- certificate
- certification
- certified
- certify
- certifying
- classification
- classified
- classify
- classifying
- falsify
- fortify
- glorified
- glorify
- horrify
- identification
- identified
- identify
- identifying
- intensify
- justifiable
- justification
- justified
- justify
- modify
- mystify
- pacifist
- pacifying
- personify
- qualify
- scientific
- significant
- signify
- simplified
- simplify
- simplifying
- terrific
- terrify
- terrifying
- unification
- unified
- unify
- unjustifiable
- verification
- verified
- verify

ign
- benign
- malignant

il
- peril

ile
- versatile
- versatility

im
- immigrant
- immigrants
- immigrate
- impartial
- impediment
- impersonal
- impersonate
- implying

in
- import
- importance
- important
- imported
- importing
- improved
- improvement
- improving

image
- imaginary
- imagination
- imaginations
- imaginative
- imagine

in
- include
- inclusive
- incoherent
- inconceivable
- inconsiderate
- inconsistent
- increases
- incredible
- incurable
- indefinite
- indefinitely
- indescribable
- indict
- indicted
- indictment
- indispensable
- individual
- inexperienced
- infection
- infer
- inference
- inferred
- inferring
- infinite
- infinitely
- influence

Word Parts

in

- influenced
- influential
- influenza
- inform
- informal
- information
- informative
- informing
- infuriate
- injection
- innumerable
- inquire
- inquired
- inquiries
- inquiring
- inquiry
- inquisitive
- insects
- insist
- insisted
- insistent
- inspect
- inspection
- inspector
- inspiration
- inspire
- instant
- instantaneous
- instructor
- intensify
- invasion
- invent
- inversion
- invincible
- invisible
- involvement
- misinformed
- twin
- twins
- uninformed

industry
- industrial
- industry

ine
- disciplinary
- discipline
- imaginary
- imagination
- imaginations
- imaginative
- imagine
- medicine
- wolverine

inter
- interceded
- interest
- interesting
- intermission
- interrupt
- interruption

intro
- introduce
- introduced
- introduction

ion
- audition
- absorption
- accommodation
- accommodations
- action
- actions
- administration
- admission
- affection
- affectionate
- application
- appreciation
- association
- assumption
- authorization
- benediction
- calculations
- caution

ion

- certification
- characterization
- citation
- civilization
- classification
- collection
- commotion
- companion
- competition
- comprehension
- compression
- concentration
- concentrations
- conception
- conclusion
- conclusions
- confusion
- conservation
- consideration
- consumption
- contradiction
- conversation
- corruption
- creation
- deception
- decision
- deduction
- definition
- depreciation
- description
- deviation
- dictation
- diction
- dictionaries
- dictionary
- direction
- division
- duration
- elevation
- equation

Word Parts

ion

erosion
eruption
exclamation
exclusion
execution
exhaustion
expansion
expectation
expedition
explanation
extension
extraction
identification
imagination
imaginations
infection
information
injection
inspection
inspiration
intermission
interruption
introduction
invasion
inversion
justification
location
malediction
manifestation
migration
misconception
motion
multiplication
nutrition
objectionable
observation
occasion
occasional
occasionally

occasions
organization
perception
permission
persuasion
precaution
preconception
prediction
prescription
presentation
presumption
proclamation
production
profession
professional
projection
promotion
provision
punctuation
question
questionable
questioned
questionnaire
questions
quotation
radiation
reaction
rebellion
reception
reduction
registration
rejection
relationship
repetition
reservation
respiration
reunion
revelation
reversion

revision
separation
station
stationery
subscription
summarization
summation
supervision
suspension
television
translation
transmission
unification
union
unquestionable
vacation
verification
version
vision

ious

cautious
conscientious
curiosity
curious
expeditious
gracious
graciousness
judicious
laborious
malicious
nutritious
sacrilegious
spacious
suspicious
vicious
viciousness
vivacious

ique

antique
mystique
technique

Word Parts

ique
- unique
- uniqueness

ir
- irrelevant
- irresponsible

irrit
- irritable
- irritate
- irritated

ise
- advertise
- chastise

ish
- boyish
- establish
- establishment
- finish
- reestablish
- selfishness

isk
- asterisk

isle
- isle
- island

ism
- criticism
- mechanism
- rheumatism

ist
- bicyclist
- characteristic
- chemistry
- geologist
- pacifist
- physicist
- scientist
- sophisticated

it
- auditor
- credit
- exit
- spirit
- spiritual
- summit
- transit

- unit
- visit
- visitor
- visitors

ite
- competition
- competitor
- competitors
- definite
- definitely
- definition
- expedite
- expedition
- expeditious
- finite
- graphite
- hesitancy
- hesitant
- hesitate
- indefinite
- indefinitely
- infinite
- infinitely
- inquisitive
- nutrition
- nutritious
- opposite
- repetition
- reunite
- unite
- united
- veritable

ity
- ability
- activity
- actuality
- authority
- capability
- commodity
- compatibility
- curiosity

ive

- density
- desirability
- disability
- durability
- generosity
- hospitality
- humanity
- humidity
- identity
- legality
- majority
- monstrosity
- opportunities
- opportunity
- originality
- personality
- possibility
- priority
- probability
- quality
- quantity
- reality
- responsibility
- simplicity
- stability
- stupidity
- unity
- variability
- versatility
- visibility

ive
- activity
- adhesive
- apprehensive
- automotive
- cohesive
- conclusive
- consecutive
- deceptive
- decisive

Word Parts

ive

- deductive
- descriptive
- disruptive
- effective
- effectively
- excessive
- excessively
- exclusive
- execute
- exhaustive
- expensive
- expressive
- imaginative
- inclusive
- informative
- inquisitive
- locomotive
- motive
- objective
- offensive
- perceptive
- persuasive
- prescriptive
- radioactive
- receptive
- resistive
- responsive
- submissive
- unappreciative

ize
- agonize
- antagonize
- apologize
- apologized
- authorization
- authorize
- categorize
- characterization
- characterize
- civilization
- civilize
- criticize
- decentralize
- equalize
- familiarize
- hospitalize
- hospitalized
- localize
- mechanize
- memorize
- modernize
- organization
- patronize
- patronizes
- personalize
- personalized
- realize
- socialize
- summarization
- summarize
- symbolize

ject
- deject
- injection
- object
- objected
- objectionable
- objective
- project
- projection
- projector
- rejected
- rejection
- subject

joy
- enjoy
- enjoyable
- enjoyed
- enjoyment
- joyful
- joyous

judge
- judging
- misjudge
- misjudged
- prejudge

judice
- judicial
- judicious
- prejudice
- prejudicial

juice
- juice

just
- justice
- justifiable
- justification
- justified
- justify
- unjustifiable

knife
- knife

knive
- knives

knot
- knots
- knotted

know
- acknowledge
- acknowledged
- knowledge
- knowledgeable

lab
- lab

labor
- collaborate
- elaborate
- laboratory
- laborious

lack
- lack

late
- lately
- relationship
- translate
- translation

lay
- relay

Word Parts

leak

leak	leakage		believer		technology
	leaked		believes		theology
	leaking		believing	**lone**	lone
lect	collection		relieve		loneliness
ledge	acknowledge		relieved	**lot**	allotment
	acknowledged		relieves		allotted
	knowledge	**light**	enlightening	**love**	love
	knowledgeable		unenlightened		lovely
lege	legality	**like**	like	**low**	allowed
	legible		likelihood	**luck**	luckier
	sacrilege		likely		luckiest
	sacrilegious		likeness		lucky
length	lengthy	**lique**	oblique	**luxe**	deluxe
less	blameless	**list**	list		luxurious
	breathless		listings		luxury
	breathlessness	**lit**	litter	**ly**	abruptly
	careless	**loco**	allocate		actually
	effortless		dislocate		athletically
	formless		local		awfully
	hopeless		localize		barely
	hopelessly		locate		busily
	meaningless		location		casually
	spotless		locomotive		coarsely
	starless		relocate		completely
	valueless	**loge**	apologize		constantly
leve	elevation		apologized		correctly
	elevator		apology		critically
	irrelevant		astrologer		currently
	lever		astrology		definitely
	relevance		biology		directly
	relevant		geologist		duly
lief	belief		geology		effectively
	disbelief		logic		equally
	relief		morphology		exceedingly
lieve	believable		ornithology		excessively
	believe		psychology		finally
	believed		radiology		fluently

ly

Word Parts

ly

	friendliest
	friendliness
	friendly
	graphically
	greatly
	happily
	hopefully
	hopelessly
	indefinitely
	infinitely
	lately
	likelihood
	likely
	loneliness
	lovely
	manly
	manually
	modestly
	mysteriously
	obviously
	occasionally
	partially
	physically
	quietly
	really
	sadly
	sorely
	strangely
	thoroughly
	truly
	unanimously
	unfortunately
	unusually
	yearly
mad	madness
magic	magic
	magical
	magician
main	maintain

major	major
	majority
male	malady
	malediction
	malevolent
	malice
	malicious
	malignant
man	manly
mani	manicure
	manifestation
	manipulate
manu	manage
	manageable
	managed
	management
	manager
	managerial
	manual
	manually
	manufacture
	manufacturer
	manuscript
	mismanage
	mismanaged
many	many
marry	marriage
	married
	marry
	marrying
	remarried
mean	meaningless
	meanings
	meant
mechan	mechanic
	mechanical
	mechanics

ment

	mechanism
	mechanize
medic	medicine
meet	meeting
melan	melancholy
meme	memorize
mend	recommend
	recommendation
	recommended
ment	allotment
	amusement
	argument
	arrangement
	basement
	commitment
	department
	departmental
	embarrassment
	enjoyment
	entertainment
	equipment
	establishment
	experiment
	experimental
	impediment
	improvement
	indictment
	involvement
	management
	movement
	nutriment
	replacement
	requirement
	resentment
	sacrament
	sentimental
	shipment
	statement

migra   myst

migra	emigrant	**miscell**	miscellaneous		modern
	emigrate	**mise**	compromise		modernize
	emigrated	**miss**	admission		modest
	immigrant		intermission		modestly
	immigrants		omissions		modesty
	immigrate		permissible		modify
	immigration		permission	**monster**	monster
	migrant		submissive		monstrosity
	migrants		transmissible		monstrous
	migrate		transmission	**morpho**	morphograph
	migration	**mit**	admit		morphographs
	migratory		admittance		morphology
milit	militant		admitted	**mote**	automotive
	military		admitting		commotion
minister	administration		commit		demote
mire	admirable		commitment		locomotive
	admire		committed		motion
mis	mischief		committee		motive
	mischievous		noncommittal		motor
	misconceive		omit		promoted
	misconception		omitted		promotion
	misfortune		permit		promoter
	mishap		permitted		remote
	mishaps		permitting	**move**	move
	misinformed		remittance		movement
	misjudge		submit	**multi**	multiplication
	misjudged		submitted		multiply
	mismanage		transmit		multiplying
	mismanaged		transmitting	**muse**	amusement
	misnomer	**mode**	accommodate		amusing
	misplaced		accommodation		museum
	misspell		accommodations		music
	misspelling		commodity		musician
	misspells		mode	**myst**	mysterious
	mistake		model		mysteriously
	mistaken		moderate		mystery
	mistakes		moderation		mystical
	mistral		moderator		

Word Parts

myst
    mystify
    mystique

nasty
    nastiest
    nasty

naut
    astronaut
    cosmonaut

nerve
    nervous

ness
    breathlessness
    business
    businesses
    forgiveness
    friendliness
    graciousness
    happiness
    heaviness
    likeness
    loneliness
    madness
    sadness
    selfishness
    soreness
    strangeness
    uniqueness
    viciousness

new
    new

nice
    nice

nin
    forty-ninth
    ninety-ninth
    ninth

nine
    nineteen
    ninetieth
    ninety
    ninety-five
    ninety-fourth
    ninety-ninth

noise
    noise
    noisier
    noisy

nome
    astronomer
    astronomers
    astronomical
    astronomy
    economic
    misnomer

non
    noncommittal
    nonexistent

note
    notice
    noticeable
    unnoticed

nox
    equinox

numer
    enumerate
    innumerable
    numeral
    numerical
    numerous

nutri
    nutrient
    nutriment
    nutrition
    nutritious

o
    omissions
    omit
    omitted

ob
    object
    objected
    objectionable
    objective
    observation
    obvious
    obviously

oc
    occasion
    occasional
    occasionally
    occasions
    occur
    occurred
    occurrence
    occurrences
    occurs

of
    offensive
    offer
    offered
    offering
    office
    official

on
    espionage
    patron
    patronage
    patronize
    patronizes

one
    cyclone

onym
    anonymous
    antonym
    synonym
    synonymous

op
    opportune
    opportunities
    opportunity
    opposite

or
    actor
    auditor
    benefactor
    competitor
    competitors
    conductor
    creator
    dictator
    educator
    elevator

Word Parts

or — **pat**

	equator
	extractor
	factories
	inspector
	instructor
	memorize
	moderator
	motor
	originator
	projector
	promoter
	radiator
	supervisor
	survivor
	terror
	tremor
	visitor
	visitors
organ	organization
origin	origin
	original
	originality
	originally
	originate
	originator
	unoriginal
ornitho	ornithology
ory	laboratory
	migratory
ot	patriot
	patriotic
	patriots
other	another
our	our
ous	advantageous
	anonymous
	anxious
	conscious
	continuous
	courageous
	dangerous
	desirous
	disastrous
	extraneous
	famous
	furious
	generosity
	generous
	glorious
	hazardous
	horrendous
	instantaneous
	joyous
	luxurious
	miscellaneous
	mischievous
	monstrosity
	monstrous
	mysterious
	mysteriously
	nervous
	numerous
	obvious
	obviously
	outrageous
	poisonous
	precious
	previous
	ridiculous
	simultaneous
	spontaneous
	strenuous
	stupendous
	superfluous
	synonymous
	tremendous
	unanimous
	unanimously
	unconscious
	vacuous
	various
	virtuous
	wondrous
out	outrage
	outrageous
paci	pacifist
	pacifying
pack	package
	packed
	packing
pand	expand
panse	expansion
pany	accompaniment
	accompany
	companies
	companion
	company
para	paragraph
pare	compare
	prepared
	separate
	separation
part	department
	departmental
	impartial
	partial
	partially
	parting
pass	passage
	passed
	passport
pat	patting

Word Parts **249**

Word Parts

pate — **picnic**

pate	compatibility	**pend**	expend	**period**	period
	compatible		suspend	**person**	impersonal
patri	patriarch	**pense**	compensate		impersonate
	patriot		expense		personal
	patriotic		expenses		personality
	patriots		expensive		personalize
	patron		indispensable		personalized
	patronage		suspension		personify
	patronize	**people**	people		personnel
	patronizes	**per**	antiperspirant	**pete**	compete
pear	appear		perceive		competent
	appearance		perceived		competition
	appeared		perception		competitor
	appearing		perceptive		competitors
	disappear		perfect		repetition
	disappearance		performance	**philo**	philosophical
	disappeared		performances		philosopher
	disappearing		performed		philosophy
	pear		performer	**phone**	symphony
	pears		performing		telephone
peat	repeat		perhaps	**phono**	phonograph
pedi	expedient		permissible	**photo**	photograph
	expedite		permission		photographer
	expedition		permit		photographic
	expeditious		permitted		photographs
	impediment		permitting		photography
	pedal		persecute	**phrase**	phrase
	pedestrian		persistent		rephrase
	pedicure		persuade		rephrased
pel	compelled		persuasion	**physic**	physical
	compelling		persuasive		physically
	dispel		pertaining		physician
	propel	**peri**	experience		physicist
	propeller		experiment		physics
	propelling		experimental	**physique**	physique
	repel		inexperienced	**picnic**	picnic
	repelled		peril		
	repellent				

pity

pity	pitiful		comply		reports
	pity		complying		support
place	misplaced		implying		supported
	place		multiplication		transport
	placing		multiply		transporting
	replaceable		multiplying		unreported
	replacement		pliable	**pose**	opposite
	replacing		replica		suppose
plain	explain		replied	**poss**	possibility
plan	plan		supplies		possible
	planned		supplying	**pray**	prayer
	planning	**point**	disappoint	**pre**	precaution
	plans		disappointed		precede
	unplanned	**poison**	poison		preceded
plane	explanation		poisoned		precedence
plant	plants		poisoning		precedent
	transplant		poisonous		preceding
play	play	**police**	police		preconception
	played	**port**	airport		predict
	player		deport		predictable
	playful		deported		predictably
please	pleasant		export		predicting
	pleasure		exports		prediction
	unpleasant		import		prefer
plete	completely		importance		preferable
plot	plotted		important		preference
ply	appliance		imported		preferred
	applicable		importing		preferring
	applicant		opportune		prefers
	application		opportunities		prefix
	applied		opportunity		prehistoric
	apply		passport		prejudge
	applying		port		prejudice
	compliance		portable		prejudicial
	complicate		porter		prepared
	complied		report		prescribe
			reported		prescription
			reporter		prescriptive

pre

Word Parts

pre

	present
	presentation
	presented
	presumption
	previewing
	previous
preci	appreciable
	appreciate
	appreciation
	depreciate
	depreciates
	depreciation
	precious
	unappreciative
prehend	apprehend
	comprehend
prehense	apprehensive
	comprehension
press	compress
	compressible
	compression
	expressive
	pressure
prin	principal
	principles
prior	priority
prise	enterprise
	surprise
pro	compromise
	procedure
	proceed
	proceeded
	proceeding
	proceedings
	proceeds
	process
	proclamation
	produced
	production
	profess
	profession
	professional
	project
	projection
	projector
	promoted
	promotion
	promoter
	propel
	propeller
	propelling
	prosecute
	protected
	provision
	unprotected
proach	approach
	approached
probe	probability
	probably
propi	propriety
prove	improved
	improvement
	improving
psycho	psychology
pule	manipulate
pulse	pulsate
punctu	punctual
	punctuate
	punctuation
	puncture
pute	computer

quit

quaint	acquaintance
	acquainted
quale	qualify
	quality
quant	quantity
quer	conquer
quere	queries
	query
quest	conquest
	question
	questionable
	questioned
	questionnaire
	questions
	request
	unquestionable
quiet	quieted
	quieter
	quietly
quip	equip
	equipment
	equipped
quire	acquire
	acquired
	acquiring
	inquire
	inquired
	inquiries
	inquiring
	inquiry
	require
	required
	requirement
quise	inquisitive
quit	acquit

Word Parts

quit
- acquittal
- acquitted
- acquitting
- quitter
- quitting

quiz
- quiz
- quizzed
- quizzes
- quizzical
- quizzing

quote
- quotation
- quote
- quoted

race
- race
- racing

radio
- radial
- radiant
- radiate
- radiation
- radiator
- radioactive
- radiology

rage
- outrage
- outrageous

rain
- raining

range
- arrangement

re
- irrelevant
- irresponsible
- reaction
- rebel
- rebellion
- rebels
- recede
- receding
- receive
- received
- receiver
- receiving
- reception
- receptive
- recommend
- recommended
- recovered
- recur
- recurred
- recurrence
- recurrences
- recurrent
- recurring
- recurs
- reduced
- reducible
- reduction
- reestablish
- refer
- reference
- referral
- referred
- referring
- refining
- reformed
- refusal
- refuse
- refused
- regretful
- regrettable
- rejected
- rejection
- relationship
- relay
- relevance
- relevant
- relief
- relieve
- relieved
- relieves
- relocate
- remarried
- remittance
- remote
- repeat
- repel
- repelled
- repellent
- repetition
- rephrase
- rephrased
- replaceable
- replacement
- replacing
- replica
- report
- reported
- reporter
- reports
- request
- require
- required
- requirement
- resent
- resentment
- reservation
- residents
- resist
- resistant
- resisted
- resistible
- resistive
- resourceful
- respect
- respectable
- respiration
- response
- responsibility

Word Parts

re scribe

	responsible	**rhyme**	rhyme	**sacri**	sacred
	responsive		rhymed		sacrifice
	reunion		rhyming		sacrificial
	reunite	**rhythm**	rhythm		sacrilege
	reusable		rhythmic		sacrilegious
	revelation		rhythmical	**sad**	sadder
	reversal	**ridicule**	ridicule		saddest
	reverse		ridiculed		sadly
	reversible		ridiculous		sadness
	reversion	**rise**	arise	**safe**	safety
	reviewer	**rob**	robber	**sake**	forsake
	revised		robberies		forsaken
	revision	**rode**	erode	**sample**	sampled
	revival	**rose**	erosion	**sandal**	sandal
	revived	**rough**	rough	**sandwich**	sandwich
	revolve	**round**	around		sandwiches
	revolver		surrounding	**save**	save
	unreported	**rrhea**	rhinorrhea	**say**	saying
real	real	**run**	runner		says
	reality		running	**scheme**	schematic
	realize		runny		scheme
	really	**rupt**	abrupt		scheming
rect	correctly		abruptly	**school**	school
	direct		bankrupt		schooling
	direction		corrupt	**sci**	conscience
	directly		corruptible		conscientious
register	register		corruption		conscious
	registration		disruptive		science
rely	reliable		eruption		scientific
rest	rest		interrupt		scientist
rhetor	rhetoric		interruption		unconscious
	rhetorical		rupture	**scope**	telescope
rheum	rheumatism	**ry**	chemistry	**scribe**	describable
rhino	rhino	**sacra**	sacrament		describe
	rhinoceros				
	rhinorrhea				

254 Word Parts

scribe

	describes		sentimental	**sire**	desirability
	prescribe	**serve**	conservation		desirable
	subscribe		observation		desire
script	descript		reservation		desirous
	description		server		undesirable
	descriptive		service	**sist**	consist
	manuscript		serviceable		consisted
	prescription	**shine**	shiny		consistency
	prescriptive	**ship**	relationship		consistent
	subscription		ship		exist
	transcript		shipment		existence
se	separate		shipper		inconsistent
	separation		shipping		insist
sect	insects	**shop**	shopper		insisted
secu	consecutive		shoppers		insistent
	execute		shopping		nonexistent
	execution		shops		persistent
	executive	**should**	should		resist
	persecute	**show**	showed		resistant
	prosecute		shows		resisted
	second	**side**	residents		resistible
seem	seemed	**sider**	consider		resistive
self	selfishness		considerable	**sit**	sitting
semi	semicircle		considerably	**skin**	skinny
	semicolon		consideration	**slam**	slammed
sense	sensible		inconsiderate	**snap**	snap
sent	absent	**sign**	signal		snapped
	consents		signed	**so**	whatsoever
	dissent		significant	**soci**	antisocial
	present		signify		associate
	presentation	**simple**	simplicity		association
	presented		simplified		dissociate
	resent		simplify		sociable
	resentment		simplifying		social
	sent		simply		socialize
	sentence	**simult**	simultaneous		societies
	sentenced				society

Word Parts

some   **strenu**

some	wholesome		expire		reestablish
	worrisome		inspiration		stability
son	unison		inspire		stable
soph	philosophical		perspire		state
	philosophy		respiration		statement
	sophisticated		spiral		station
sorb	absorbed		spirit		stationary
sore	sorely		spiritual		stationery
	soreness	**spise**	despise		substantial
	sorer	**spond**	respond	**star**	starless
	sorest	**sponse**	irresponsible	**start**	started
sorpt	absorption		response	**stay**	staying
source	resourceful		responsibility	**step**	step
space	spacious		responsible		stepped
spect	expect		responsive		stepping
	expectation	**spont**	spontaneous	**stir**	stir
	expected	**spot**	spotless		stirred
	expecting		spotted	**stop**	stopping
	inspect	**spray**	spray	**store**	storage
	inspection	**spy**	espionage		stored
	inspector		spied		storing
	respect		spy	**story**	historian
	respectable		spying		historic
spell	misspell	**sta**	constant		historical
	misspells		constantly		history
	misspelling		distance		prehistoric
	spellings		distances		stories
spend	spending		equidistant		story
sphere	atmosphere		establish	**stove**	stove
	hemisphere		establishment	**strange**	strangely
spice	conspicuous		instant		strangeness
	suspicious		instantaneous		stranger
spire	antiperspirant				strangest
	conspire			**strenu**	strenuous

256   Word Parts

Word Parts

strophe — **tele**

strophe	apostrophe		summary		swimmers
stroy	destroyed		summation		swimming
struct	instructor		summed		swims
study	studied		summit	**sym**	symphony
	studies		sums	**symbol**	symbol
	study	**sume**	assumed		symbolic
	studying		consume		symbolize
stupe	stupendous		presume		symbols
	stupid	**sumpt**	assumption	**syn**	synonym
	stupidity		consumption		synonymous
sturdy	sturdiest		presumption	**tail**	curtail
su	suspicious	**sun**	sunnier	**tain**	contain
suade	persuade		sunniest		contained
suase	persuasion		sunny		container
	persuasive	**sup**	supplies		entertain
sub	sub		supplying		entertainer
	subject		support		entertainment
	submissive		supported		maintain
	submit		suppose		pertaining
	submitted	**super**	superfluous	**take**	mistake
	subscribe		supervise		mistaken
	subscription		supervision		mistakes
	substantial		supervisor		taken
suc	succeed	**sur**	surface		takes
	succeeded		surfaced	**techno**	technical
	succeeding		surprise		technique
	success		surrounding		technology
	successful		survivable	**tect**	protected
	unsuccessful		survive		unprotected
suf	suffer		survived	**teen**	fifteen
	suffered		survivor		fourteen
	suffering		survivors		fourteenth
sum	summarization	**sus**	susceptible		nineteen
	summarize		suspend	**tele**	telegraph
			suspension		telephone
		swim	swimmer		

Word Parts

tele
	telescope
	televise
	television
tend	extend
	intend
tene	tenuous
tense	extension
	intensify
tent	discontent
ter	deter
	terrible
	terrific
	terrify
	terrifying
	terror
th	fifth
	forty-ninth
	fourteenth
	fourth
	growth
	health
	healthier
	healthy
	ninety-ninth
	ninth
	truth
	truthful
	twelfth
	unhealthy
theo	theology
they	they
thief	thief
thieve	thievery
	thieves
think	think
thorough	thorough
	thoroughly
thought	thought
	thoughtful
through	through
time	time
tinue	continue
	continued
	continuous
	discontinue
toy	toy
	toys
trace	trace
	traceable
	tracing
tract	extraction
	extractor
	tract
trade	trades
	trading
trans	transfer
	transferred
	transform
	transformed
	transit
	translate
	translation
	transmissible
	transmission
	transmit
	transmitting
	transplant
	transport
	transporting
trap	trapped
	trapping

ty
treme	tremendous
	tremor
tri	triangle
	tricycle
	trivial
trim	trim
trip	tripped
trol	control
	controlled
	controlling
	uncontrollable
true	true
	truly
	truth
	truthful
try	mistrial
	trial
	tried
	trying
tw	between
	twelve
	twenty
	twenty-two
	twice
	twilight
	twin
	twins
	two
twelf	twelfth
twelve	twelve
ty	casualty
	duty
	fifty
	forties
	fortieth
	forty

Word Parts

ty
- forty-four
- forty-ninth
- ninetieth
- ninety
- ninety-five
- ninety-ninth
- safety
- twenty
- twenty-two

ual
- actuality
- actually
- casual
- casually
- casualty
- eventual
- individual
- spiritual
- unusual
- unusually
- usual
- visual

um
- museum
- vacuum

un
- unaffected
- unappreciative
- unbreakable
- unconscious
- uncontrollable
- uncover
- undefined
- undeniable
- undeniably
- undesirable
- undiscovered
- unenlightened
- unfixed
- unforgettable
- unfortunate
- unfortunately
- unhappy
- unhealthy
- uninformed
- unjustifiable
- unnoticed
- unoriginal
- unplanned
- unpleasant
- unprotected
- unquestionable
- unreported
- unsuccessful
- unusual
- unusually

une
- fortunate
- fortune
- misfortune
- opportune
- opportunities
- opportunity
- unfortunate
- unfortunately

uni
- reunion
- reunite
- unanimous
- unanimously
- unicycle
- unification
- unified
- uniform
- unify
- union
- unique
- uniqueness
- unison
- unit
- unite
- united
- unity
- universal
- universe

uous
- conspicuous
- tenuous

up
- whereupon

ure
- creature
- enclosure
- failure
- manufacture
- manufacturer
- pleasure
- pressure
- procedure
- puncture
- rupture

ury
- luxurious
- luxury

us
- chorus

use
- reusable
- unusual
- unusually
- usable
- usage
- useful
- usual

ute
- consecutive
- execute
- execution
- executive
- persecute
- prosecute

vacu
- evacuate
- evacuated
- vacancy
- vacant

Word Parts

vacu

	vacate
	vacation
	vacuous
	vacuum
vade	invade
vale	equivalence
	equivalent
	valid
value	valuable
	valueless
van	van
vant	advantage
	advantageous
	disadvantage
vary	variability
	variable
	variance
	varied
	variety
	various
	varying
veal	reveal
vase	invasion
vele	revelation
vent	event
	eventual
	invent
verse	conversation
	converse
	inversion
	reversal
	reverse
	reversible
	reversion
	universal
	universe

	versatile
	versatility
	verse
	version
vert	advertise
	convertible
very	verification
	verified
	verify
	very
vet	vet
via	deviate
	deviation
	obvious
	obviously
	previous
	trivial
	viaduct
vice	advice
	vice
	vicious
	viciousness
vide	divide
	divided
	divider
	individual
	provide
view	previewing
	reviewer
vince	convincible
	invincible
virtue	virtue
	virtuous
vise	advise
	advised
	devise

ware

	divisible
	division
	invisible
	provision
	revised
	revision
	supervise
	supervision
	supervisor
	televise
	television
	visibility
	visible
	vision
	visit
	visitor
	visitors
	visual
vive	revival
	revived
	survivable
	survive
	survived
	survivor
	vivacious
	vivid
voice	voice
vole	benevolent
	malevolent
volve	involvement
	revolve
	revolver
vote	voter
wait	wait
	waited
	waiter
ware	warehouses

wash — year

wash	washer	**where**	whereas	**wonder**	wonderful
waste	waste		whereupon		wondrous
	wasteful	**white**	whitest	**work**	worker
wax	waxier	**who**	whoever		workers
	waxiest	**whole**	whole		working
	waxy		wholesome	**worry**	worried
weak	weak	**whom**	whomever		worrisome
	weaker	**wide**	widest		worry
week	weeks	**wife**	wife		worrying
weigh	weigh	**winter**	winter	**wrap**	wrapper
	weighed	**wit**	wittier		wrappers
	weight		wittiest		wrapping
wel	welcome		witty		wrappings
were	were	**wive**	wives		wraps
what	whatever	**wolf**	wolf	**write**	write
	whatsoever	**wolve**	wolverine		writer
when	when		wolves	**year**	yearly
					years

Study Lists

1–5

acquire
across
action
airport
autobiography
autograph
barely
biography
changing
decided
deport
discontent
expensive
export
exports
famous
final
forgiven
formal
fortunate
graphic
great
greatly
hopeful
hopelessly
hoping
imagination
important
informal
inquire
introduce
lately
likely
likeness
lovely
misinformed
misjudged
misspell
mistaken
morphograph
performance
photographer
photographic
portable
porter
really
reformed
replacement
replacing
report
reported
require
requirement
reusable
should
showed
support
supported
telegraph
television
their
tracing
transform
translate
transmit
transplant
transport
transporting
uncover
uninformed
unreported
usable
usage
widest
wonderful

6–10

admirable
admire
amusement
athletic
athletically
baggage
basement
basic
bibliography
changing
civilize
confusing
conscientious
critically
criticism
deduction
dispel
excessively
expressive
formless
geography
gotten
graphite
hats
hopeless
hottest
inquiring
interest
inversion
knots
madness
magic
medicine
notice
package
partial
parting
patting
people
perceptive
photograph
photography
physicist
placing
pleasure
poisonous
pulsate
realize
sadness
sitting
snapped
spotted
starless
storage
stranger
surprise
swimmer
telescope
trades
trading
translation
transmission
tripped
valuable
valueless
washer
whitest

11–15

acknowledge
admission
advised
appearance
appeared
baggage
bagging
beautiful
blameless
buried
careless
carriage
copied
covered
crying
denial
devise
diseased
drying
easy
embarrassed
enjoyment
failure
fanciest
fateful
fatty
friendly
glorious
haphazard
happen
happiness
happy
heaviest
hurrying
impartial
improved
incurable
joyous
judging
justice
leakage
leaked
leaking
manufacture
married
mishap
mishaps
mistake
mistakes
movement
packed
packing
perhaps
pitiful
planning
playful
racing
refining
revision
runner
runny
sadder
saddest
sadly
saying
shiny
shipped
shipping
shopper
skinny

Study Lists

slammed
sorely
soreness
sorer
sorest
staying
stepped
stored
storing
strangely
strangeness
strangest
studying
sturdiest
televise
thoroughly
toys
trial
tried
trying
unusually
varied
version
vision
visitor
worried

16–20

accommodate
admit
athletics
baker
bakes
baking
boxer
burial
business
casual
commit
commitment
compelling
copying
denying
embarrassment
enjoyed
fitness
friendliest
happier
happiest
happily
hazardous
hidden
imaginary
improvement
informative
inquired
invisible
luckier
luckiest
lucky
manufacturer
mothering
noisier
omit
paragraph
permit
pleasant
propel
receive
repellent
shopping
shops
skipped
sprayed
stopping
sunnier
sunniest
sunny
supervision
swimming
swims
unfixed
unpleasant
usual
wittier
wittiest
witty
worrisome
wrapper
wrapping
wraps

21–25

accommodation
actually
another
applied
astronomer
biggest
casualty
commodity
complying
concur
consistent
critic
critical
currency
current
durable
duration
during
endurance
endure
fantasies
fantasy
funny
hemisphere
imagine
inconsistent
knotted
likelihood
misfortune
model
moderate
modern
modernize
modest
occasion
occasionally
occur
philosopher
planned
recur
rephrased
stepping
stirred
various
visit
worrying

26–30

admittance
advise
allotment
allotted
allowed
anchored
approach
backache
begin
beginner
beginning
characteristic
chemical
chemistry
chords
chorus
committee
controlled
curtail
differ
disaster
disciple
discipline
echoes
excel
excelled
excellence
excellent
exercising
ferry
forbid
forbidden
forgive
forgot
forgotten
forsake
forsaken
growth
healthy
industrial
knowledge
loneliness
marriage
mechanical
mechanism
melancholy
military
modesty
occurrence
offer
omitted
origin
original
permitting
plants
preferred
propeller
propelling
purse
recurring
refer
safety
schematic
schooling
sound
suffer
technology
transfer
transferred
uncontrollable
unhappy
very
visual

31–35

anonymous
belligerent
benediction
bicycle
businesses
citation
concurred
concurrence
concurs
conductor

Study Lists

contradict
contradiction
controlling
dictation
dictator
diction
dictionary
disappoint
disciplinary
edict
educate
familiar
forth
hymnal
hypnenated
hysterical
impersonal
impersonate
indict
indictment
magician
malediction
manage
manual
manuscript
mysterious
mystical
occurred
occurs
personality
personalize
personify
physician
predict
prediction
probable
production
question
rebellion
received
receiver
recommended
recurred
recurrence
recurrent

recurs
reduced
regrettable
rhythmical
site
surrounding
symbolic
synonym
synonymous
unforgettable
unquestionable

36–40

acknowledged
activity
adequate
admitting
appearing
beam
bridge
characterization
close
compelled
conceivable
conception
create
deceive
deceived
deceptive
density
describe
description
discoveries
earlier
enduring
equal
equation
equator
equidistant
equinox
equivalent
find
forties
fortieth

forty
forty-one
four
fourteen
fourteenth
fourth
fury
hole
importance
importing
indescribable
inquiry
inscribe
inscription
list
misconceive
misconception
mystery
opportunity
perceive
perception
performing
permissible
predictable
preferring
prescribe
prescription
rebels
receptive
recommend
regretful
rejection
scripture
separate
story
submissive
submit
subscribe
subscription
summarization
summarize
summary
summation
summed
summit

sums
unenlightened
variance
varying
weak
yearly

41–45

antecedent
asterisk
breathlessness
clothes
conversation
created
creation
creature
descriptive
earliest
enclosure
exceed
exceeded
excessive
furious
healthier
inconceivable
indispensable
infuriate
involvement
mysteriously
observation
perceived
precede
precedence
prepared
prescriptive
presentation
previewing
proceed
quotation
raining
recede
reception
referring
refusal

remarried
semicolon
simply
stories
succeed

46–50

concede
conceded
concedes
dictionaries
divide
exceeding
exceedingly
exercises
familiarize
individual
meaningless
meant
omissions
opposite
preceded
precedent
preceding
procedure
proceeded
proceeding
proceedings
receding
remittance
resentment
reservation
rhetoric
rheumatism
rhinoceros
rhubarb
rhyme
rhymed
rhyming
rhythm
rhythmic
scheming
sentence
succeeded

Study Lists

succeeding
surfaced
symphony
transit
transmitting
weight
weighted

51–55

affect
between
clouds
coarse
compare
confined
constant
contrary
define
definite
definitely
definition
deviate
distance
equate
event
eventual
finally
finish
finite
indefinite
indefinitely
infinite
instant
manicure
manifestation
manipulate
mismanage
obvious
opportune
pressure
previous
profess
puncture
sacred
sacrifice

sacrificial
sacrilege
sacrilegious
sentenced
stable
state
statement
station
surface
trivial
twelve
twenty
twice
twilight
twin
undefined
viaduct
weather

56–60

advice
armor/armour
behavior/
   behaviour
center/centre
color/colour
conclusive
emigrate
equally
establish
evacuate
favor/favour
favorite/favourite
glamor/glamour
gray/grey
harbor/harbour
honor/honour
humor/humour
immigrant
immigrate
labor/labour
migrant
migrate
migratory
mold/mould

museum
music
neighbor/
   neighbour
obviously
odor/odour
patriarch
patriot
patriotic
patron
patronage
patronize
plough/plow
principal
program/
   programme
punctual
punctuate
radial
radiant
radiate
radiation
radioactive
radiology
reversal
sacrament
studied
telephone
tire/tyre
vacancy
vacant
vacate
vacuous
vacuum
valor/valour
vapor/vapour
variable

61–65

aisle
benefactor
beneficial
benefit
benevolent
benign

carrying
classified
classify
clearance
coarsely
departmental
equivalence
expedient
expedition
falsify
horrify
identify
impediment
intensify
justify
malady
malice
malicious
malignant
managerial
modify
musician
mystify
nutrient
nutriment
nutrition
nutritious
pedal
pedestrian
pedicure
qualify
reaction
reestablish
reporter
sale
signify
simplicity
simplified
simplify
simplifying
stationery
terrify
two
unjustifiable

66–70

acquainted
acquired
acquittal
acquitted
affection
autobiographical
autobiography
cautious
challenge
classifying
compete
competition
competitor
competitors
conscience
conscious
conspicuous
continued
continuous
deviation
disappearance
equipment
equipped
espionage
expedite
experience
experiment
fort
gracious
graciousness
identified
inexperienced
knight
migration
noncommittal
office
official
peril
quieted
quitter
quitting
quizzed
quizzical

Study Lists

quoted
sandwich
sandwiches
science
scientific
scientist
spacious
spied
strenuous
tract
vacation
verse
vicious
virtue
virtuous

71–75

accounted
accounting
acquiring
application
apply
applying
central
compliance
comply
concentrate
counted
counting
curious
decentralize
deluxe
dislocate
eccentric
entertain
fortify
grammar
injection
local
locate
location
locomotive
luxurious
luxury
maintain

multiply
objective
pertaining
profession
programmer
programming
project
projection
projector
quizzing
refused
rejected
relocate
replica
separation
subject
successful
tenuous
unprotected
viciousness

76–80

absent
affectionate
appliance
beggar
elevation
enumerate
experimental
identifying
innumerable
irrelevant
lever
manually
marrying
nervous
numeral
numerical
numerous
pair
pliable
relevance
relevant
ridicule
ridiculed

ridiculous
suspicious
tremendous
tremor
unsuccessful
wait
waiter
waste
wasteful
weighed
wholesome

81–85

abrupt
abruptly
agonize
applicant
bankrupt
beautify
caravan
categorize
certificate
certifying
competent
container
correctly
corrupt
corruption
course
deter
effect
entertainment
eruption
exam
examination
examine
friendliness
glorify
gymnasium
historian
historic
history
implying
influenza
inspection

inspector
interrupt
laboratory
multiplying
objectionable
opportunities
pacifist
robberies
rupture
sight
submarine
terrible
terrific
terrifying
terror
unconscious
undeniable
unicycle
uniform
union
unite
verify
veterinarian

86–90

affluent
bicyclist
bilateral
burying
caution
certain
certify
complicate
concert
cyclic
cyclone
disruptive
effective
effort
effortless
equilateral
fluent
fluid
historical
influence

interruption
justification
lateral
multiplication
pacifying
prehistoric
reunite
spying
superfluous
supplying
tricycle
unaffected
unanimous
unification
unify
unique
unison
unit
unity
universal
universe
versatile
versatility

91–95

accompaniment
animal
antagonize
antibodies
antibody
antiperspirant
antisocial
antonym
categories
cautions
certification
certified
companies
compensate
consistency
denied
fluently
identification
influential
insistent

Study Lists

isle
judgment/
    judgement
judicial
judicious
justifiable
justified
misjudge
precaution
prejudge
prejudice
prejudicial
principle
respectable
reunion
significant
stationary
studies
substantial
unified
verification
verified

96–100

appreciable
appreciate
apprehensive
automotive
commotion
comprehension
conclusion
consecutive
conservation
conspire
decision
defensive
demote
depreciate
division
erosion
except
excite
exclusive
execute
execution

exist
existence
expand
expansion
expect
expectation
expense
expire
explosive
extension
inclusive
insisted
inspiration
invasion
motion
motive
motor
offensive
originate
persecute
persistent
persuasion
philosophical
precious
professional
promote
promotion
prosecute
provision
remote
respiration
responsive
second
spirit
spiritual
suspension
too
unappreciative
week
whole

101–105

advantageous
antique
audible

believable
believe
changeable
chargeable
compatible
conclude
considerable
consist
courageous
critique
divider
exchangeable
excitable
exclamation
exclude
explanation
extraction
five
horrible
include
incredible
insist
inspire
knives
knowledgeable
manageable
mystique
noticeable
outrageous
physique
possible
proclamation
relieve
repetition
revelation
serviceable
susceptible
technique
thieves
traceable
transmissible
visible
wolves
workable

106–110

absorb
absorption
administration
angry
anxiety
associate
association
assume
assumption
authority
collaborate
confer
conference
conferred
conferring
consider
considerably
consideration
considers
consume
consumption
deduce
deodorize
desirable
desire
desires
desirous
differed
different
differing
disastrous
dissociate
elaborate
entered
entrance
entry
evaporate
extraneous
formality
forty-ninth
glamorize
hindrance
humanity

humorous
hungrily
hungry
inconsiderate
inference
inferred
inferring
instantaneous
introduction
laborious
miscellaneous
monstrous
nine
nineteen
nineteenth
ninetieth
ninety
ninety-five
ninth
offered
offering
preferable
preference
presume
presumption
product
propriety
reality
reduce
reduction
reference
referral
referred
registration
rigorous
simultaneous
sociable
social
societies
society
spontaneous
suffered
suffering
twenty-ninth
undesirable

Study Lists 267

Study Lists

vaporize
variety
wondrous

111–115

actual
actuality
adhere
adhered
adherent
adhesive
analogy
anthropology
apologize
applicable
astrology
audience
audition
author
biology
capable
capacity
chronology
coherent

cohesive
conquer
credible
deception
deniable
entomology
fifty
forty-four
geology
hesitant
hesitate
hospitable
hospital
hospitality
human
humid
humidity
incoherent
irritable
irritate
legal
legality
logic
major

majority
morphology
nineteen
originality
ornithology
prefers
prior
priority
psychology
replaceable
sociology
stupid
stupidity
theology

116–120

advertise
apology
argument
authorization
authorize
awful
awfully
chastise

compatibility
compressible
compression
computerize
corruptible
curiosity
deductible
deductive
desirability
difference
disability
duly
durability
duty
exhaustible
exhaustion
exhaustive
formalize
generosity
geologist
hospitalize
legalize
monstrosity
organization

organize
possibility
prefer
probability
resistible
resistive
responsibility
responsible
reversible
reversion
revival
revive
sensible
stability
survivable
survive
survivor
truly
truth
truthful
visibility
vivacious
vivid

Spelling Rules

Lesson	Rule	Explanation
3	Final-E Rule	When do you drop the final **e** from a word? When the next morphograph begins with a vowel letter.
7	Doubling Rule (Short Words)	When do you double the final **consonant** of a short word? When the word ends **cvc** and the next morphograph begins with a **vowel letter.**
12	Y-to-I Rule	When do you change the **y** to **i** in a word? When a word ends with a consonant-and-**y** and the next morphograph begins with anything except **i.**
28	Doubling Rule (Long Words)	When a word ends in a short **cvc** morphograph use the doubling rule.
51	Final-Vowel Rule (Part 1)	*There are two parts to this rule. The first part of the rule is introduced in Lesson 51:* Drop the final vowel from a morphograph when the next morphograph begins with a vowel. *This rule covers morphographs that end in* **e**, *such as* **muse + ic = music.** *It also covers other vowels:* **vacu + ate = vacate.**
58	Final-Vowel Rule (Part 2)	*In Lesson 58 the second part of the final-vowel rule is given:* Drop the final vowel when the next morphograph begins with a vowel UNLESS YOU HEAR BOTH VOWEL SOUNDS. *In the word* **museum** *you hear the vowels* **e** *and* **u,** *so you keep the final vowel,* **e.** *In the word* **evacuate,** *you hear the vowels* **u** *and* **a,** *so you keep the final vowel,* **u.**
84	Final-Vowel Rule (Final Y)	Drop the final **y** when a word ends consonant-and-**y** and the next morphograph begins with **i,** unless you hear both vowel sounds. *In the word* **crying,** *you hear the vowel for* **y** *and for* **i,** *so you keep the final vowel,* **y.** *In* **glory + ify = glorify,** *you cannot hear both vowels, so the* **y** *drops.*
97	E-X Rule	Drop the **s** from the beginning of a morphograph when that morphograph follows **ex.**
107	F-E-R Doubling Rule	Double the **r** if **fer** is stressed. *In the word* **referred, fer** *is stressed, so you double the* **r.** *In the word* **reference, fer** *is not stressed, so you don't double the* **r.**
112	I-T-Y Rule	Drop the **u** when you combine **ous + ity = osity.** Add an **i** when you combine **able + ity = ability.** Add an **i** when you combine **ible + ity = ibility.**

Facts About Morphographs

1. All morphographs follow spelling rules.
2. All morphographs have meaning.
3. Morphographs are the smallest word parts that have meaning.
4. Some words have only one morphograph.
   Some words have more than one morphograph.

	1	2	3	4	5	6
A	re**port**	photo**graph**ic	in**quire**	trans**form**	**trans**plant	re**tain**
B	im**port**ed	**graph**	ac**quire**	**form**al	**trans**mit	con**tain**er
C	**port**	tele**graph**	re**quire**ment	unin**form**ed	**trans**porting	ob**tain**able
D				per**form**ance	**trans**late	enter**tain**

Contractions

Component Words	Contractions
are not	aren't
can not	can't
could not	couldn't
did not	didn't
do not	don't
does not	doesn't
have not	haven't
he had	he'd
he is	he's
he will	he'll
here is	here's
I am	I'm
I will	I'll
it is	it's
let us	let's
she had	she'd
she is	she's
she will	she'll
should not	shouldn't

Component Words	Contractions
that is	that's
they are	they're
they had	they'd
they have	they've
they will	they'll
was not	wasn't
we are	we're
we had	we'd
we have	we've
we will	we'll
were not	weren't
what is	what's
who is	who's
would not	wouldn't
you are	you're
you had	you'd
you have	you've
you will	you'll

Homonyms

affect	refers to:	make something change
	example:	The coarse clouds will *affect* the weather.
effect	refers to:	outcome
	example:	The moon has an *effect* on the tides.
aisle	refers to:	a row
	example:	The suitcase was blocking the *aisle*.
I'll	refers to:	I will
	example:	*I'll* be there at noon.
isle	refers to:	an island
	example:	Let's move to a tropical *isle*.
ate	refers to:	eat in the past
	example:	I *ate* a sandwich.
eight	refers to:	the number 8
	example:	The dog had *eight* puppies.
bare	refers to:	without covering; empty
	example:	In the winter some trees are *bare*.
bear	refers to:	a certain animal or to support
	example:	The huge *bear* drank from a stream. The bridge can't *bear* more weight.

close	refers to:	shut something
	example:	Please *close* the door.
clothes	refers to:	things you wear
	example:	They bought lots of *clothes*.
coarse	refers to:	rough and ragged
	example:	The old dog's fur was *coarse*.
course	refers to:	path or route you follow
	example:	The plane changed *course* because of the storm.
desert	refers to:	leave or abandon
	example:	I wouldn't *desert* a friend in need.
dessert	refers to:	food served at the end of a meal
	example:	We had ice cream for *dessert*.
feat	refers to:	something hard to do
	example:	Climbing the mountain was a great *feat*.
feet	refers to:	body part
	example:	Her *feet* were sore from running.
for	refers to:	in place of
	example:	She went to the store *for* me.
four	refers to:	the number 4
	example:	Cats have *four* legs.

hear	refers to:	listen
	example:	I can't *hear* you.
here	refers to:	this place
	example:	Come over *here*.
hole	refers to:	empty space
	example:	I have a *hole* in my sock.
whole	refers to:	entire; complete
	example:	He ate the *whole* pie.
it's	refers to:	it is
	example:	*It's* raining
its	refers to:	belonging to it
	example:	The dog chased *its* tale.
loan	refers to:	allow to borrow something
	example:	She will *loan* me lunch money.
lone	refers to:	by itself
	example:	There was a *lone* tree.
marry	refers to:	wed or unite
	example:	She said she would *marry* Steve.
merry	refers to:	happy, full of fun
	example:	The hikers were a *merry* group.
meat	refers to:	food from animals
	example:	Some people don't eat *meat*.
meet	refers to:	come together
	example:	We agreed to *meet* next week.

no	refers to:	negative answer
	example:	*No*, I'm not going.
know	refers to:	understand or be familiar with
	example:	We *know* how to sail.
peace	refers to:	calm; no war
	example:	I like *peace* and quiet.
piece	refers to:	a part
	example:	I ate a *piece* of fruit.
pear	refers to:	a certain fruit that grows on a tree
	example:	Mom put a *pear* in my lunch.
pair	refers to:	two of a kind
	example:	Mack got a new *pair* of basketball shoes.
plain	refers to:	simple; ordinary
	example:	She wore a *plain* black dress.
plane	refers to:	flat surface or air transportation
	example:	The *plane* landed safely.
principal	refers to:	the person who runs a school
	example:	Our *principal* keeps the school running smoothly.
principle	refers to:	a rule
	example:	Telling the truth is an important *principle*.

Homonyms

Homonyms

right	refers to:	correct or opposite of left
	example:	All my answers were *right*. She wears a ring on her *right* hand.
write	refers to:	put words on paper
	example:	You must *write* neatly.
sail	refers to:	travel on water in a ship or a boat
	example:	We learned how to *sail* at camp.
sale	refers to:	available to buy, or an offer at a cheaper price
	example:	Our house is for *sale*. He bought the shoes on *sale*.
scene	refers to:	view or setting
	example:	It was a painting of an ocean *scene*.
seen	refers to:	see in the past
	example:	I have *seen* that picture.
sew	refers to:	join with a needle and thread
	example:	He will *sew* a new button on his coat.
sow	refers to:	plant seeds
	example:	Farmers *sow* their fields in the early spring.

site	refers to:	place or location
	example:	We are building a house on this *site*.
sight	refers to:	seeing, vision or view
	example:	A dog's sense of smell is better than its sense of *sight*.
some	refers to:	not all; an indefinite number
	example:	*Some* of my friends were there.
sum	refers to:	the total amount
	example:	The *sum* of two and ten is twelve.
stationary	refers to:	something that doesn't move
	example:	She exercises on a *stationary* bike.
stationery	refers to:	paper for writing letters
	example:	His *stationery* had his address on it.
tail	refers to:	the back end
	example:	The dog chased his *tail*.
tale	refers to:	a story
	example:	He told an interesting *tale*.
their	refers to:	belonging to them
	example:	It is *their* house.
there	refers to:	that place
	example:	Go over *there*.
they're	refers to:	they are
	example:	I think *they're* ready.

Homonyms

threw	refers to:	throw in the past
	example:	She *threw* the ball.
through	refers to:	in one side and out the other
	example:	We went *through* the tunnel.
to	refers to:	at or toward
	example:	She walked *to* school.
too	refers to:	also
	example:	Why don't you come along, *too*?
two	refers to:	the number 2
	example:	I ate *two* apples.
vary	refers to:	change
	example:	His moods *vary* from day to day.
very	refers to:	really, quite, especially
	example:	That story is *very* imaginative.
waist	refers to:	a person's mid-section
	example:	She wore a belt around her *waist*.
waste	refers to:	throw away
	example:	Don't *waste* the food.
wait	refers to:	delay or expect something
	example:	We had to *wait* an hour for the bus.
weight	refers to:	heaviness
	example:	He felt like he had the *weight* of the world on his shoulders.

ware	refers to:	product for sale
	example:	The baker sold his *wares*.
wear	refers to:	have clothes on your body
	example:	What shall I *wear* today?
where	refers to:	what place
	example:	*Where* do you want to go?
weather	refers to:	what it feels like out of doors
	example:	Always wear a hat cold *weather*.
whether	refers to:	if
	example:	I don't care *whether* I go or not.
weak	refers to:	the opposite of strong
	example:	The wrestler felt *weak* after the match.
week	refers to:	seven days
	example:	We go on vacation next *week*.
wood	refers to:	what trees are made of
	example:	We need *wood* for the fire.
would	refers to:	what might happen
	example:	I *would* like to go to Paris.
your	refers to:	belonging to you
	example:	*Your* coat is blue.
you're	refers to:	you are
	example:	*You're* early.

Test Charts

	Lesson 5	Lesson 10	Lesson 15	Lesson 20	Lesson 25	Lesson 30	
Super Speller	25	25	25	25	25	25	**30-Lesson Total**
	24	24	24	24	24	24	
	23	23	23	23	23	23	
Very Good Speller	22	22	22	22	22	22	**138 = Super Speller**
	21	21	21	21	21	21	
	20	20	20	20	20	20	
	19	19	19	19	19	19	
	18	18	18	18	18	18	
	17	17	17	17	17	17	
	16	16	16	16	16	16	
	15	15	15	15	15	15	
	14	14	14	14	14	14	
	13	13	13	13	13	13	
	12	12	12	12	12	12	
	11	11	11	11	11	11	
	10	10	10	10	10	10	
	9	9	9	9	9	9	
	8	8	8	8	8	8	
	7	7	7	7	7	7	
	6	6	6	6	6	6	
	5	5	5	5	5	5	
	4	4	4	4	4	4	
	3	3	3	3	3	3	
	2	2	2	2	2	2	
	1	1	1	1	1	1	

Test Charts

	Lesson 35	Lesson 40	Lesson 45	Lesson 50	Lesson 55	Lesson 60
Super Speller	25	25	25	25	25	25
	24	24	24	24	24	24
	23	23	23	23	23	23
Very Good Speller	22	22	22	22	22	22
	21	21	21	21	21	21
	20	20	20	20	20	20
	19	19	19	19	19	19
	18	18	18	18	18	18
	17	17	17	17	17	17
	16	16	16	16	16	16
	15	15	15	15	15	15
	14	14	14	14	14	14
	13	13	13	13	13	13
	12	12	12	12	12	12
	11	11	11	11	11	11
	10	10	10	10	10	10
	9	9	9	9	9	9
	8	8	8	8	8	8
	7	7	7	7	7	7
	6	6	6	6	6	6
	5	5	5	5	5	5
	4	4	4	4	4	4
	3	3	3	3	3	3
	2	2	2	2	2	2
	1	1	1	1	1	1

30-Lesson Total

138 = Super Speller

Test Charts

	Lesson 65	Lesson 70	Lesson 75	Lesson 80	Lesson 85	Lesson 90
Super Speller	25	25	25	25	25	25
	24	24	24	24	24	24
	23	23	23	23	23	23
Very Good Speller	22	22	22	22	22	22
	21	21	21	21	21	21
	20	20	20	20	20	20
	19	19	19	19	19	19
	18	18	18	18	18	18
	17	17	17	17	17	17
	16	16	16	16	16	16
	15	15	15	15	15	15
	14	14	14	14	14	14
	13	13	13	13	13	13
	12	12	12	12	12	12
	11	11	11	11	11	11
	10	10	10	10	10	10
	9	9	9	9	9	9
	8	8	8	8	8	8
	7	7	7	7	7	7
	6	6	6	6	6	6
	5	5	5	5	5	5
	4	4	4	4	4	4
	3	3	3	3	3	3
	2	2	2	2	2	2
	1	1	1	1	1	1

30-Lesson Total

138 = Super Speller

Test Charts

	Lesson 95	Lesson 100	Lesson 105	Lesson 110	Lesson 115	Lesson 120	
Super Speller	25	25	25	25	25	25	**30-Lesson Total**
	24	24	24	24	24	24	
	23	23	23	23	23	23	
Very Good Speller	22	22	22	22	22	22	**138 = Super Speller**
	21	21	21	21	21	21	
	20	20	20	20	20	20	
	19	19	19	19	19	19	
	18	18	18	18	18	18	
	17	17	17	17	17	17	
	16	16	16	16	16	16	
	15	15	15	15	15	15	
	14	14	14	14	14	14	
	13	13	13	13	13	13	
	12	12	12	12	12	12	
	11	11	11	11	11	11	
	10	10	10	10	10	10	
	9	9	9	9	9	9	
	8	8	8	8	8	8	
	7	7	7	7	7	7	
	6	6	6	6	6	6	
	5	5	5	5	5	5	
	4	4	4	4	4	4	
	3	3	3	3	3	3	
	2	2	2	2	2	2	
	1	1	1	1	1	1